To my father

Brian O'Neill

1927 - 2008

ACKNOWLEDGEMENTS

I am deeply grateful for all the people and experiences in my life, which have enabled me to do the work described in Complete Union and subsequently to write the book. Since my initial study of Psychology, which began in Pennsylvania thirty years ago, at age eighteen, my career and my professional colleagues have been a source of continuous joy and fulfilment. I have been fortunate to have excellent teachers, mentors, therapists, and supervisors. To all of you whose names I hold in my heart, I thank you.

On a personal level, I would like to acknowledge my parents, Brian and Bridget O'Neill, who provided a good, wholesome environment for their eleven children and were my first teachers about life and relationships.

My husband, Patrick, also deserves a special mention for his ongoing support, encouragement, and practical help.

Extracts from 'Let's Talk Sex' by Davina McCall and Anita Naik, published by Channel 4 Books are reprinted by kind permission of The Random House Group Ltd.

I very much appreciate the help of Steven Weekes and Garrett Bonner at Original Writing for their editing support and advice about the book.

Finally, I would like to thank all my clients, who place their trust in me and allow me the honour of walking with them for some of life's journey. I especially thank Tina and Darren for the privilege of accompanying them and for their great generosity in allowing me to write and publish their story.

INTRODUCTION

THIS BOOK IS THE STORY OF MY WORK with a couple who were married for six years and had never had sexual intercourse. It is a detailed inside view of the process of therapy told by the three people involved: firstly, myself as the therapist, guiding the healing process; secondly, the woman called Tina, who came from deep pain to joyous union with her own body, her sexuality, and her husband; and thirdly, the man called Darren, who waited patiently, supported, and participated in the healing journey. For all three of us, there were challenges, surprises, and much learning. We were each enriched by our time together. I hope that my description captures the great working relationship we developed and the shared joy as each stage of progress was achieved.

For me, it has been a great honour to work with two beautiful people, to feel their pain, accompany them in their struggles, and celebrate their triumphs. They will go forward without me now. Our work together is finished. We have all been changed by it.

The decision to write this book was made at the end of the therapy in discussion with the couple who hope their story may help others. In addition, it is my hope that the honest description of the therapy process, so seldom written, and possibly never to date in the Irish context, will be of use to other therapists and in training institutions. I have intentionally written this book as a story rather than as any kind of academic treatise. I hope that in doing so, it will be easily readable and that the warmth of the counselling relationship and the very human journey to healing will shine through the pages. The couple have given me written permission to write and publish their story. Names and other identifying details have been changed to protect their identity. Apart from that, this is a very accurate account of the therapy process.

▌Therapeutic Approach

Tina seemed to be suffering from a condition called "Vaginismus, " which is defined by Chaplin in his Dictionary of Psychology (p.521) as follows: "a painful and involuntary contraction of the muscles associated with the vagina. The disorder may prevent coitus and is believed to be the result of psychological factors." Because I generally see labels as unhelpful, I did not mention this term when working with the couple. I simply set out to help them to achieve their goal of developing a sexual relationship. While other therapists might use different methods of treating the problem and have equal success, I drew on the resources available to me from my years of training and experience.

Traditional sex therapy, as formulated by Masters and Johnson, works on healing sexual problems by halting sexual contact while the therapist prescribes increasing levels of pleasurable touching which over time culminates in full sexual intercourse. The basic philosophy is that, once the sexual relationship is functioning well, the underlying psychological blocks or issues automatically heal. Psychotherapy, on the other hand, believes that the brain is the biggest sexual organ, and that by healing old wounds, negative programming, and inaccurate bodily knowledge, a person can become free to express joyous sexuality.

In my therapy with Darren and Tina, I combined the above two approaches, along with elements of other therapies, including bibliotherapy, hypnotherapy, visualisation, and Reiki healing. Essentially, I operated in a creative mode of drawing on any knowledge and skills which I believed would be helpful as each week of the therapy unfolded. This way of working kept the process interesting and dynamic, and much healing occurred. As well as achieving their stated goal of having an enjoyable sexual relationship, the couple grew in awareness and learned a lot which will support them in their lives.

▌ Layout of Book

Once I get into describing the process of therapy, each session is written as a chapter. Firstly, I include Tina's journal written during the weekly or fortnightly interval. Secondly, I add Darren's journal. And finally, I detail the main themes of the counselling hour. The journals are included exactly as the couple wrote them with the occasional exception of very slight changes to protect their identity.

▌ Initial Contact

At the end of March 2007, at the suggestion of his G.P., Darren phoned me to make an appointment for himself and his wife. In our brief telephone conversation, he told me they were married for almost six years and his wife had never been able to have sex. My initial reaction was one of interest and excitement at the challenge for me as therapist, in addition to some concern about the duration of the problem, knowing that I would be helping this couple to break a long-standing habit in their relationship. I asked them both to attend the first session.

THE FIRST MEETING
30TH MARCH 2007

IN EVERY FIRST MEETING, be it with an individual client, a couple, or a family, my task is to get to know the person and gather as much background information as possible. I am noticing how people look, how their eye contact is, how a couple relate to one another and to me, as well as gathering as much information as possible about the presenting problem. All the while, I am formulating tentative hypotheses about the psychological causes of the problem and how I might intervene to help. The session with Darren and Tina was like this. The following is a description of my impressions.

The couple were in their mid-thirties and from a rural area of south east Ireland. They were average in most respects: height, weight, physical attractiveness etc. When they took their seats in my therapy room, I introduced myself, assured them of confidentiality, and wrote their personal details into my client file. They were both in good health, using no medication, and had no history of psychiatric problems. Neither had ever spoken to a counsellor before this.

When I asked them to tell me what they needed from psychotherapy, Darren said they had been married for almost six years and Tina had never been able to have sexual intercourse. I turned to Tina and asked her to say something about that. Her face cracked in deep pain, she started to cry and stood up and moved toward the door saying, "I can't do this." I calmly asked her to sit down and assured her that she was here to get help and that I would do all in my power to help her. I acknowledged her pain and stated that it can initially be very difficult to talk about sexual problems because they are so personal. I stressed that everything we talked about was confidential and that first sessions are often the most difficult and reassured her that eventually she would feel more comfortable, once she got to know me.

We continued the first session getting information about their meeting, courtship, and the general state of their marriage. As a couple, they were physically affectionate, regularly hugging and kissing. On a sexual level, Darren had previously had sexual intercourse with a couple of partners, prior to meeting Tina. Tina had never had sexual intercourse and had failed to allow penetration of the vagina during an attempted smear test, sometime before her marriage. Tina was comfortable allowing Darren to manually stimulate her clitoris and bring her to orgasm. However, she would become very anxious at any attempt to penetrate her vagina either manually or with his penis. Also, she had never brought Darren to orgasm, so he relied solely on self-masturbation for his sexual release.

I explained to the couple that the therapy would require a serious commitment on their part: weekly attendance for several months. I asked that they would stop all sexual contact, except kissing and hugging, for a few weeks to take the pressure off while Tina initially attended alone to work through some of her psychological blocks. After that, my plan was to work with the couple together to gradually build a sexual relationship by meeting specified goals, which we would agree together at that stage. I said that I thought the process would take at least four months (in hindsight overly optimistic). They said they had booked a holiday for September, and I replied that there was a chance they would be able to have sex by then. I wanted to instil hope without giving any guarantees, because therapy is a process over which I have little control.

I explained to Tina that I needed to rule out the possibility that there was any physical cause for her inability to have sex, such as a tight hymen or any other impediment. I therefore requested that she attend her G.P for examination. She decided to attend Darren's G.P., since he was the one who had referred them to me. It was obvious to me that Tina had very little language with which to talk about sexual matters in addition to being extremely uncomfortable with the topic. I therefore coached her on some questions to ask her

G.P. She agreed to attend her appointment before her next visit with me.

Before the end of the session, I requested that Tina stop on her way home and buy a nice hardback notebook in which to journal each week during the therapy. I suggested she chose a pretty coloured notebook which would honour her input, and I asked her to write her impressions and feelings about our first session as well as anything she had learned. I explained that the journal would allow her an outlet between sessions for her thoughts and feelings. In addition, it would record her learning in a very tangible way, which would allow her in the weeks and months ahead to look back on her own progress. I said that each week, I would ask her to share her journal with me, so that we could discuss its contents and use it as a resource in the therapy process.

I was aware at the end of the session that part of my work with this couple was to completely re-educate them about sex and replace negative, unhelpful messages with truthful statements. The written journal would be a means of catching negative thoughts and actually challenging them and having Tina examine them and, if helpful, rewrite them.

I asked Tina to attend alone for the next session, and I suggested that Darren could drive her or accompany her if he wished. Tina said she wished to come alone, and I saw that as a very positive sign of her commitment to help herself.

It is my usual policy to end all my therapy sessions with a brief visualisation of approximately three minutes. This has a number of benefits for the client or couple. Firstly, it helps to calm and centre the person before leaving. Secondly it gives a formal close to our work. Thirdly and, perhaps most importantly, the visualisation helps to bring in light and healing into the energetic spaces left empty by the client having talked about the problems and released stored emotions. I sincerely believe this visualisation contributes to the healing that happens for clients in therapy sessions with me. I vary the wording slightly each time to make the visualisation directly relevant to each client and their particular sharing in that session.

In the work with Tina and Darren, the visualisation may have sounded something like this: "As you sit in your chairs now at the end of our time together, I would like you to close your eyes and imagine that, by sharing your thoughts and experiences here, you have created an empty space in your head and taken some pressure off your mind. I would also like you to imagine that, by releasing your feelings, you have created an empty space in your chest and stomach area. Then I would like you to visualise a golden light coming down from the sun, shining in through the top of your head, filling your mind with peace, positive thinking, and the ability to see clearly the issues that are helpful for you to address in therapy. Allow that golden light to shine down over your face into your throat and allow it to fill your chest and stomach, bringing in to your emotional body feelings of peace, calmness, hope, and courage to face the difficulties in your life and take steps to heal them. Let the light shine into the cells in your physical body, bringing good health, energy, and vitality, and bringing a lot of healing and love into your sexual organs. Then allow the golden light to fill your aura, the energy field around your body, forming a protective bubble of golden light all around you, keeping you safe and strong. Take a deep breath now and breathe in peace, breathe out fear. Again, breathe in peace, breathe out fear. For a third time, breathe in peace, breathe out fear. And then gently open your eyes."

SESSION TWO
5TH APRIL 2007

TINA WAS EARLY FOR THE SESSION and looked a lot more relaxed than a week earlier. During the therapy, it was a joy for me to notice that as Tina freed herself of her burdens and constrictions about her sexuality, she became prettier and more joyful.

I began by reading Tina's journal from the previous week. As suggested, she had chosen a hard-back brightly coloured journal with red and orange vegetables on the cover. I had informed her the previous week that orange is the colour associated with the second chakra or energy centre in the body, and this energy centre feeds the sexual organs. Wearing orange thus stimulates this chakra. I was therefore pleased with her choice of journal.

The following is Tina's Journal entry exactly as she wrote it:

30th March 2007: Shared/talked about a major problem in our marriage.

Got advice on what to do i.e. where to go (doctor).

Weight lifted off my shoulders and a feeling of relief.

Excited that I may be able to have sex with Darren.

Be able to change the way I think about sex.

To live a normal life like other couples.

Finally doing something about not having sex.

Like opening a door that has been closed for so long.

The problem has been put to the back of my mind for years.

A feeling of being sick, nervous and frightened before meeting with Alice, also doctor, but great relief afterwards.

If I can do this, I can do anything. It's the hardest thing I ever had to do in my life.

OUR MEETING TOGETHER:

I was pleased that Tina had cooperated in obtaining and writing the journal. I complimented her on her efforts. I also pointed out that there were very few complete sentences in this journal entry. It was as if she was talking about a problem outside herself. I therefore took each line of her entry and demonstrated how to make sentences by putting the subject "I" before each line. I explained to her that this would help her to feel more involved and to take greater responsibility for her progress in therapy. This is how the revised entry read the following week:

> I shared/talked about a major problem in our marriage. I got advice on what to do i.e. where to go (doctor). It was a weight lifted off my shoulders—a feeling of relief. I am excited that I may be able to have sex with Darren. I want to be able to change the way I think about sex and to live a normal life like other couples. I am finally doing something about not having sex. It's like opening a door that has been closed for so long. I had put the problem to the back of my mind for years. I had a feeling of being sick, nervous, and frightened before meeting with Alice, also doctor, but a great relief afterwards. If I can do this, I can do anything. It's the hardest thing I ever had to do in my life.

You, the reader will see Tina's growth in the journaling as we go along. This was the only time I suggested any rewriting of it.

I then asked Tina to tell me about her week. Even though she was aware of an unknown journey ahead, she was hopeful now about addressing her sexual problems. She had attended her male doctor who had recommended a smear test to be performed by a female nurse in the surgery the following week. That gave me the opportunity to explain to Tina exactly what would happen during the smear test and to mentally prepare her for it. I believed the experience of the smear test was very important in that a success would be a step forward whereas any trauma could reinforce her fears. I lay in the carpeted floor of my office with my knees raised and showed Tina how to do pelvic tilts. I demonstrated that pushing the small of her back into the floor or the doctor's couch would tilt her pelvis back and allow easier access to her vagina. I also suggested that she breathe deeply during the insertion of the speculum to relax the muscles at the entrance to the vagina. I also told her that this position would be the easiest for her when she eventually started to have sexual intercourse. I suggested she practice doing these pelvic tilts at home to get her body used to the position.

I explained to Tina that the smear test is a slightly unpleasant experience for most women. I described the speculum which is a metal device like a cone inserted into the vagina and gradually expanded to give the nurse or doctor access to the cervix or entrance to the womb. I suggested that Tina ask the nurse to run warm water on the speculum to heat it up as this makes penetration easier. Some doctors, but not all, automatically do this.

Tina had attempted a smear test about seven years ago . At that time, she had no idea as to what to expect and became so tense as the doctor attempted to insert the speculum that the doctor quickly abandoned the procedure telling her there was no need for it since she was not sexually active. I was concerned that another negative experience now could further convince Tina of her inability to allow penetration of the vagina, whereas a more positive experience this time round would build her confidence and give her hope.

We then discussed Tina's sexual development and the messages she had picked up about sexuality from those around her during her formative adolescent years. There was minimal sex education in the convent school Tina had attended and very little in the home apart from her mother giving her a booklet to read and asking an aunt to tell her about periods. Tina could not remember the arrival of her first period, which is unusual for a woman, as this tends to be such a major event in adolescence. She thought she was in secondary school at the time, and remembered that some of her friends had their periods before her. She also recalled being given free samples of sanitary towels and tampons in school. Tina had tried to use a tampon on a couple of occasions, but did not know where to insert it and had hurt herself by trying to insert it near her clitoris.

Tina had never studied biology, and, even now, she had very little knowledge of the human reproductive system. She was reared in a very religious Catholic family and had a close relationship with her paternal grandmother who lived with the family. Though sex was never spoken about within the family, the attitude conveyed was that sex was "dirty" and the human reproductive organs "shameful." An example of how Tina picked up these messages was that her grandmother would switch off the television when anything sexual was shown. Unusually, Tina had not shared with her girlfriends about her developing sexuality, so there was no counter view to the one absorbed at home.

I realised that part of my work with Tina was to re-educate her about her own female body and her sexuality. In this session and in nearly all subsequent sessions, I spoke very honestly in a "woman to woman fashion," giving information, challenging false unhelpful notions and reinforcing healthier and more balanced perceptions. I explained that all parts of the human body are equally beautiful and made for the tasks they perform. Why then should a person feel ashamed of the sexual organs? I explained that part of Tina's healing was to get to know her own body and get comfortable with it. This would be the foundation for getting comfortable with her husband's body and for being relaxed in letting him explore her body.

As a homework assignment, I asked Tina to run a nice bubble bath and soak in it. While in the bath, I asked her to touch her own body, her arms, her legs, her neck and her sexual organs. I asked her to gently feel with her fingers the entrance to her vagina and where it lay in relation to the rest of her private parts. Tina initially seemed very uncomfortable with this request. I encouraged her to share her discomfort and found it to be related to earlier Catholic teaching that touching one's own body is sinful. Again I challenged this flawed belief by asking, "If God created every part of your body, how could it be any more sinful to put your finger into your vagina than it is to put your finger into your mouth or your ear?" Tina could see the logic in this explanation and agreed to undertake the initial exploration of her own vagina.

At the end of this session, Tina was a more relaxed and hopeful woman. We were now at the early stages of our work together. Our communication had been comfortable that day and Tina now had some definite tasks to perform in order to move a little closer to her goal of being able to have sexual intercourse with her loving husband. As she left the therapy room, she spontaneously gave me a kiss, which surprised me, but I interpreted it as a sign of her relief and gratitude. I possibly seemed uncomfortable with this gesture of affection, as she didn't kiss me again until Christmas! Tina actually was a warm and affectionate woman and not at all like the stereotypical image of the "frigid" woman as someone cold and rigid. During the entire therapeutic relationship, I purposely avoided any labels related to the sexual dysfunction. I simply encouraged the couple to take steps to improve their situation.

Session Two took place on Holy Thursday. I had Good Friday off work, and I went to a bookshop in Wexford to look for a suitable book to educate Tina about the workings of the female body and human sexuality. Having browsed through several books on the topic, I chose "Let's Talk Sex" by Davina McCall and Anita Naik. This book is written to help parents to educate children and teenagers about sex and has sections where the authors directly address young people. It is written in clear and simple language and has excellent diagrams of the male and female reproductive organs. Over the Easter weekend, I enjoyed reading the book, reminding myself of some facts about sexuality, and, as I read, I highlighted the sections to which I wanted Tina to pay most attention. For example, I highlighted those statements which reassured the reader that negative messages from parents and others about sex can cause young people to feel anxious about something which should be normal and natural. In addition, the book contained very realistic descriptions of first time sex as possibly uncomfortable and emphasised that good sex between two people is a learned and practised thing. Also, the book contained an excellent section about cervical smears, which confirmed what I had already shared with Tina.

Session Three
12th April 2007

Tina again arrived early and with her homework completed. We spoke for a while about her relearning of facts and attitudes about sex. She seemed open to examining and changing earlier beliefs such as: "Good girls don't enjoy sex," and "Sex is for reproduction and not enjoyment." At this point, I asked Tina if she had ever experienced any type of sexual abuse, as I knew it was essential to deal with this if it were causing her anxiety about having sex with her husband. I explained that sexual abuse can be a range of inappropriate behaviours from unwanted sexual comments, to invasive touching of breasts or genitals, to violent rape. Tina assured me that she had experienced no sex abuse of any kind, and intuitively I believed her. I also assured her that as our therapy progressed if she became aware of anything, it was important for her to feel safe in sharing it.

Tina then invited me to read her weekly journal which went

as follows:

> *I talked at the counselling about my visit to the doctor and how hard it was for me to do that.*
>
> *Alice explained what would take place when I go for my smear test on Friday morning which I really hate the thought of doing. But I am going to do it.*
>
> *I was encouraged to take a bath and relax and feel my vagina area, which was something I never had done before in my life. Because I would have thought it to be wrong to do this to oneself or as Alice put it "sinful," which is exactly how I would have felt about it.*
>
> *After much looking, I found my vagina entrance, which I never knew was so low down.*
>
> *It was all about getting to know my body and to like my body.*
>
> *Alice also explained about the vagina. It's small, but it's like an elastic band in that it can expand: i.e. for the birth of a baby.*

OUR MEETING TOGETHER:

In my view, the most striking line in Tina's journal this week

was that Tina had actually not known exactly where the

entrance to her vagina lay. She had discovered it and was

surprised by it in the bath that week. We discussed this, and Tina expressed shyness and relief about finally allowing herself to get to know her own female body. I assured her that, as she became more comfortable knowing and touching her own body, she would gradually become more comfortable allowing her husband to explore it.

To continue to familiarise herself with her own body, I asked Tina if she would be willing to look at her vagina and surrounding areas in a mirror and draw a picture of it. I said the picture did not necessarily have to be in her journal. She could keep it completely private, if she wished to do so and just talk to me about the experience. Tina said she would try anything which I thought would help her. I then suggested how she might do this exercise. Possibly the easiest method is to sit on a cushion in one's naked body facing a wall. Then raise ones knees with the legs wide apart. Prop a mirror up against the wall, and, with the hands, explore the private parts all the while carefully looking at the view in the mirror. Then with a notebook nearby, sketch the im-

age one sees, and later put some colours into the sketch using crayons or colouring pencils which can be dark or light
to indicate the depth and mystery of the vagina. I told Tina
that I had once done this myself as a homework assignment
for a sexuality workshop, and that I was completely in awe
of the beauty of the female vagina, which looks like a deli-
cate flower. I encouraged Tina to take her time with the exercise and come back and talk with me about it next week.

The appointment for Tina's smear test was the day after
this session, and again I talked Tina through the procedure
and the breathing and pelvic tilting she could do to make the
examination as easy as possible for herself. I then gave her
the copy of "Let's Talk Sex," and pointed out the section on
smear tests and other areas I had highlighted. I suggested
that Tina would read one chapter per week and make notes
of anything significant to her in her journal. We agreed that
Tina would phone me after the smear test to tell me how it
went.

SESSION FOUR
19TH APRIL 2007

TINA HAD PHONED ME straight after her smear test to tell me that, with some difficulty and a lot of patient encouragement from the female nurse, she had done it. She was delighted, and I was very pleased, as I saw it as a definite goal achieved. For the first time in her life, she had allowed an object to penetrate the vagina. It gave me hope that, in time, and with the removal of psychological blocks, and more cognitive behavioural therapy, that she would be able to allow and eventually enjoy penetration by her husband's penis.

When she came for session four, we rejoiced in the successful smear test. I shared my hope and belief with her that this was a very good omen for the outcome of her therapy. I affirmed my conviction that if she could allow the speculum, which is a quite unpleasant stainless steel object, to en-

ter her vagina, there was no reason why she could not allow
a warm penis to enter.

I then read Tina's Journal entry for that week:

> *This week was a hard week; i.e. smear test, but very
> rewarding when I actually did it.*
>
> *Had a great nurse called Sally, a very kind lady, gentle
> manner, and very understanding. Sat me down and
> talked to me. Reassured me that I wasn't alone—
> lots of help out there. But smear test was still very
> painful.*
>
> *Read first chapter of the book Alice gave me: "Let's
> Talk Sex." Found it good. Things that Alice high-
> lighted in the book are exactly what I have to do and
> think, i.e." sex is good and normal," and "our brain/
> my brain is where everything starts." A quote out of
> the book: "Children pick up messages; for instance if
> you're watching t.v. and flick channels every time sex
> comes on the screen, they'll believe sex is something
> to be embarrassed about." This is exactly what hap-
> pened in my home.*
>
> *My homework this week was to take a mirror and
> look at my vagina area etc, which I did. Alice was
> right. It was like a beautiful flower which I would
> describe as an orchid. A very detailed and delicate
> flower.*

OUR MEETING TOGETHER:

Tina had drawn her vagina in her journal and coloured it in very pretty colours of red, pink, and yellow. Again her openness about this surprised me, as it was now a normal part of our therapy for me to read her journal and discuss it. As a psychotherapist, I could have chosen to discuss with Tina her openness in showing the picture and her extreme discomfort in allowing her husband to see and explore her vagina. However, I chose instead to praise her for her efforts to complete her homework assignments, and to have her tell me her feelings as she looked at and drew her own vagina.

The major challenge for Tina in doing the exercise was to overcome her Roman Catholic guilt about the idea that touching oneself in any type of sexual way was sinful. We talked about the impact of these messages on us as woman; how such messages can distance us from being comfortable in our own bodies. Again I reiterated that every part of the human body is inherently beautiful and perfectly designed for the purposes it serves. The sexual organs serve the purposes of giving us bodily pleasure and producing babies. If one of the purposes of these organs is to give pleasure, how could it be anything but good to touch oneself and allow oneself to experience that pleasure? Then in intimate relationships, we can share that pleasure with a partner and help them to experience pleasure too.

Tina had used the image of the orchid to describe her vagina. We discussed the ways one would handle an orchid, with gentleness and reverence. Tina said Darren had always been most gentle and respectful to her. I asked Tina if any previous boyfriend had hurt or offended her in any way. She described having three boyfriends before she met Darren. Each relationship had lasted about four to six months. While there had been kissing and hugging and some fondling of breasts, Tina had always become uncomfortable with any attempt to touch her private parts. None of the boyfriends had mistreated her, but one of them put some pressure on her to have sex, and when she refused, the relationship ended. Tina had not been particularly upset by the sexual advances of any of the boyfriends, so again it seemed there was no outside trauma in her past relationships to account for her sexual problems.

Towards the end of this session, Tina told me that her sixth wedding anniversary was in the next few weeks. I asked her how she felt about that. She replied that all other anniversaries had been deeply painful for the couple in the sense that the date was a reminder that yet another year had passed and they had not succeeded in having sex. This terrible secret known only to the two of them was like an open wound in their relationship. On the one hand, Tina denied the problem to herself, convincing herself that someday it would go away. On the other hand, she felt a desperate sense of failure and almost self-hatred, telling herself that she was a "freak" and "abnormal." I reflected to her the sense of failure and loss, but I strongly encouraged her to refrain from calling herself a "freak" or other names which simply put her down and made her feel worse. As always, I said simply that she had a human problem, granted not the most common problem, but nevertheless a problem which a certain number of couples encounter. The most important thing now was that she was in the process of addressing her problems.

I could sense from Tina a huge amount of grief about the lost time in her marriage. There was not adequate time in this session to deal with the grief, but I felt she would need to release some of her sadness to make way for healing. So I encouraged her to think about her anniversary during the week and talk more to me about it next week. My opinion was that we needed to devote an entire session to the grief work.

Session Five
23rd April 2007

Tina's journal read as follows:

Talked today about our wedding anniversary—the way I used to hate it coming round as it reminded me of the fact another year was over and we had not had sex. And the years just kept coming around, and we were still no better off! But this year, I am looking forward to it as we have done something very positive about sex.

I read another chapter in my book—self esteem is a big thing which I don't have much of at times. My Dad would never praise us when we were young and still is not great at it. He criticised a lot. But I love him dearly. But in the book it says: "Self-esteem can be learnt." I am going to change negative for positive and criticism for praise.

Alice said "God will help us, but we have to help ourselves first. Then He will help us the rest of the way. But we have to make the first move ourselves."

Our Meeting Together:

Reading the journal, I acknowledged to Tina that her relationship with her father was significant to discuss, as he was the first significant man in her life, and her relationship with him probably had an influence on how she related to men in her life. Also her father's relationship to her mother most likely taught her a lot about marriage and about how men treat women. However, I suggested we come back to this at another time, as the upcoming anniversary date and her feelings about it were the most current issue.

Tina cried and released a lot of sadness about all the lost years in her marriage. Initially the couple had hoped to have several children, and each year the possibility of this was fading. She had grown to accept that she would never have children, and this was a huge loss for her. Every time a friend or relative became pregnant, Tina grieved her own loss. Every birth and christening was painful. While Tina was happy for others, she was sad for herself.

In relation to Darren, Tina was also guilty and sad. She knew she was depriving him of a normal sexual relationship. Sometimes she would say to him that he should leave her and find someone else, but deep down, she did not want that as she loved Darren and wanted to be with him. She had initially convinced herself that the problem would just go away and that the couple would have sex, but as the years slipped by, the pressure was mounting.

Tina's deepest grief was about herself as a woman. She was alienated from her own body, did not know it or understand how it worked. For years, she had told herself she was not a normal woman. She believed her body did not function in a normal way. Because she was unable to have sexual intercourse with her husband, her body would never know the joy of feeling a baby in her womb, the pain of childbirth, or the harmony of having a baby suckle her breasts. Now that she was taking steps to get more familiar and comfortable in her own body, the deep pain of years of fear and self-hatred were surfacing. As she cried and tried to put some words on her feelings, I simply stayed with her, encouraging her to breathe deeply and release her pain.

Even though such a session is very painful for the client at the time and the rawness can last for hours or even days,

I am sure from my years as a therapist, that this emotional release is the source of great healing. I reassured Tina that it was very important for her to get out this pain, so that she would not carry it for the rest of her life. She was now taking steps to move beyond her problems, and it was essential that she did not carry old regrets into the present and future. The first six years of her marriage had passed. She could not regain anything she had lost. Her feelings of regret, sadness, and guilt needed to be left behind so that she could move forward and create a joyful future. Our peace is always in the present moment. I encouraged Tina to express what needed to be expressed from her past experiences but to really focus on living in the present and to move forward from here.

The date of Tina's sixth wedding anniversary was approaching and she now had hope because she was addressing her problems. Tina said that whereas she wanted to ignore other anniversaries, she felt the couple would do something to mark this one. As always, I concluded the session by guiding Tina in the golden light visualisation to fill up the empty spaces from which she had released so much emotional pain and to move forward to seeing her seventh anniversary as one in which she would have passionate sexual intercourse with her husband. In therapy, this is called "future pacing," and has a profound impact on the subconscious mind, which believes the suggested visualisation and works to make it a reality. I used quite a lot of suggestion in this therapy, mostly just in the course of conversation. For example, I might joke with Tina as she was learning more about her body, that she would be very comfortable and competent when the time came to educate her own teenagers about sexuality. Obviously this suggested that she would have sex, give birth to children, rear them, and eventually teach them about sexuality! I fully believed all this was ahead for Tina, I wanted it for her, and I held my vision no matter how she was currently feeling in the therapy process.

Session Six
5th May 2007

TINA INITIALLY TOLD ME about her wedding anniversary and felt it was indeed the happiest and most hopeful anniversary the couple had. There was a lot of non-sexual physical affection, such as holding one another, hugging and kissing. The couple were now talking about times ahead when they would be having a sexual relationship. They had always been a unified couple, with good communication, no financial problems, positive relationships with one another's families, many meaningful friendships, fulfilling work, and a nice home. In short, the couple were well functioning in all but the sexual area of their marriage. And now, they were taking steps to heal that area.

Tina's Journal entry:

> *My last visit to Alice, I was all over the place. I was very emotional. I just can't say why I was feeling this way. Glad Darren drove me down (great support).*

Went back to see Mary, the nurse, to get my smear test results. Delighted that all was negative. She was great again, very kind.

For our anniversary, Darren and I went on the train to Dublin. We both really enjoyed our day. We were so happy to have marked our sixth anniversary.

Reading "Let's Talk Sex," I took this line out of it, "Remember, none of us ever does anything painful that doesn't give us a positive outcome."

OUR MEETING TOGETHER:

For this hour, Tina spoke in depth about her relationship with her father. He appeared to be unhappy in himself and came across as critical and negative to those close to him. He worked hard as a farmer. His mother lived with the family and had a big influence on Tina. Even though she was a loving woman, she was very traditionally religious and repressed in her attitude to sexuality. Tina's own mother worked hard inside and outside the home, and possibly was subdued in her ability to express her own personality, due to living with a negative husband and a strong mother-in law. Also, it could be more difficult for any couple to have free expression of communication whether sexual or otherwise when in-laws live with the family. Tina never saw her parents kissing or hugging or showing affection for one another.

Even up to the present day, Tina recalled her father criticising her a lot. She had felt very hurt and put down by his criticisms as a child and teenager, and even as a young adult, but in recent years, probably since getting married, moving out, and living away from him, she had been able to see his criticisms as indicators of his own negativity and unhappiness, rather than as caused by some flaw in Tina. The other significant memory of her father was his absence from the home. His whole life was work and the farm. There was little time for family. The few times when her father spent recreation time with his family stood out as Tina's happiest childhood memories. Tina was not able to tell her father anything about herself, her interests, or her feelings. She never felt important to him or valued by him.

As is common with most clients, it was difficult for Tina to say out loud the ways in which her father had hurt her. It was almost as if she was being disloyal to a man she loved. She wanted me to know that her father was essentially a good man and that she loved him and also that she knew he loved her. I reassured her that I was not interested in judging her father. My only interest was in helping her to overcome her sexual blocks, and part of that process was to understand the influence of parents on her developing sexuality and to release any hurt about it.

Why was the relationship with Tina's father relevant to her sexual problems? As the first significant male in her life, her relationship with her father had influenced her subsequent ability to relate to men on an intimate level. His criticism had made her feel less secure in herself as a person and as a woman and had made her subconsciously wary of men and mistrustful of them. He lessened her self esteem and contributed to her low opinion of herself. Sexual intercourse can be the ultimate opening of oneself to a man, and one could see that it might be difficult for Tina to give herself fully to a man when she felt deeply vulnerable in the presence of her own father.

At this point in the process, we had looked at Tina's knowledge of her own body, her sexual education, her grief about the loss of sexual expression in her marriage, and her relationships within her family of origin. While all the above issues were important and relevant, none of them on its own seemed to explain Tina's inability to allow any penetration of her vagina. My hope at this point was that by addressing some significant factors and focussing on positive changes, we would open the door for progress to be made. I felt very positive and optimistic mainly because I knew that Tina and I had developed an excellent rapport and she was very open to my suggestions.

The reader can begin to see how psychotherapy is far from being an exact science. Every human being is unique and two people with identical presenting problems can have completely different underlying causes to be addressed. I often use the analogy of a jigsaw for my work. When a client sits before me for the first time and shares a problem, the client often does not see the origin of the difficulty, and I cannot see into the client's mind to identify the causes. So I make some guesses based on my knowledge of psychology and my 23 years of work. We look at some of the client's life experiences. As the client talks about the hurts, emotions are released, and the client can begin to see the picture of how his/her life experience has brought them to this point. As several points on the jigsaw fall into place, the picture becomes clearer and clearer. It is not necessary to address every piece of the jigsaw. Often the client will accomplish much of the healing themselves once the picture is visible. Also healing in one area of the psyche will contribute to healing in other areas. In my opinion, a feeling of hope in the client is one of the essential ingredients in all healing. At difficult times in the process, the therapist must hold the vision of a successful outcome for the client. Subconsciously, the client is supported by the confidence of the therapist.

SESSION SEVEN
14TH MAY 2007

Our Meeting Together:

At this point in Tina's work, having devoted five sessions to her own psychotherapy, I decided it was important to bring her husband into the process, as ultimately, all sexual problems for a couple need to be resolved within the context of the relationship. I did not want her husband to feel left out of the process. At the same time, the individual sessions gave Tina the opportunity to look at her sexual development in the years before she met Darren. Several times later in the process when important issues came up for Tina, she always asked her husband to leave the room so that she could talk to me alone. I think the individual sessions gave her a freedom to express herself without considering her husband's feelings or reactions. She could then share with him afterwards as she felt appropriate.

Tina's Journal read as follows:

> *I spoke this week a lot about my Dad! And how he would be a very negative person. How he has a habit of criticising you on every little thing you do. But I really think he just got into a habit of doing this and knows no other way to behave. It was hard to be criticised by your father. But I was lucky to have a Granny and Mother who made up for this with lots of praise and encouragement.*
>
> *We talked about how Dad was not around much when we were young. He never had time for us, always working too hard. I do remember very well two things, our seaside trip on the 15th August and at Easter how he took time out to hide our Easter eggs around the farm, and we had to find them; " the Easter egg hunt." Very special times, as we did not have many where Dad took part. My Dad thinks the world of my siblings and me, but he just doesn't know how to show love.*
>
> *My book this week said: "Worry: you believe that sex is dirty or bad." Our upbringing can squash our enjoyment of sex. But it is "as natural and as normal as breathing."*

OUR MEETING TOGETHER:

Darren and Tina came together for session seven. It was six weeks since I had first met the couple. They looked like a happier and much more relaxed couple. Darren told me he was very proud of Tina for the work she had told him about during her five individual sessions. I explained that the purpose of the individual work was to help Tina to release old hurts and negative thought patterns which may have contributed to her fear of sex. Some of this would continue to happen in the couple sessions, but the focus now would be on using cognitive behavioural therapy to make progress in the sexual area of their marriage. Specifically this would involve the couple each week engaging in pre-agreed levels of sexual touching which in gradual stages would lead to full sexual intercourse with ejaculation.

Though I have attended brief workshops on sexuality and sex therapy over the years and read widely on the subject, I am not a sex therapist. I am a well trained and vastly experienced general therapist, and, as evident in the work with Tina and Darren, I draw on many theories and techniques in the course of my work. In Behavioural Psychology, the practitioner sets gradually increasing goals on the road toward the end goal which in this case was for the couple to have full sexual intercourse with ejaculation. As each stage is achieved, there is a rest period or a period to keep performing that behaviour until it becomes comfortable, and then one can move to the next stage. One of the challenges is to set the goals in a way that leads to definite progress without creating too much psychological anxiety for the client. Thus the goal setting is always done in collaboration with the clients.

I explained to the couple that the primary goal was to get comfortable being naked together and exploring one another's bodies in a sexual way. I asked as homework for that week that the couple would rub KY Jelly lubricant on one another's private parts. I suggested that the couple from this point forward make their sexual relationship a priority in their marriage. Thus, it would be good to chose a time when they could be at ease and unhurried and prepare for the closeness by having a shower. First Tina would massage Darren's penis and then he would massage her vagina. The goal was to kiss, hug, and show affection and then to relax, feel and enjoy the sexual touching, while also being aware of the partner's reactions. Hopefully this would gradually lead to increased intimacy between the partners.

At this point in the therapy, Tina was still too uncomfortable to go into a chemist shop and ask for KY Jelly, so I offered to buy it for her the previous week, and she paid me for it. Very soon, as she became more at ease with her sexuality, she had no trouble buying the product for herself.

I suggested to Darren to begin reading the book "Let's Talk Sex" from start to finish, as I felt it was important for him too to learn about sex and to discuss with Tina the knowledge they were acquiring. At this point, Darren said that he would also like to keep a journal each week. I had not thought about that, but I was very pleased that Darren himself came up with the idea. I interpreted it as Darren wanting to take equal part in the healing process.

Many times in my work, I make a tape of guided relaxation as a means of engaging the subconscious mind of the client in the healing process. When the client has eyes closed and is moderately relaxed, the subconscious mind is more open to positive suggestions for change. I explained this to Tina and asked that she would attend alone the following week and I would use the session to make the tape live in her presence; i.e. I would guide her through a session of relaxation focused on healing her sexuality, and I would tape the session, so that she could listen to it regularly at home between the therapy sessions.

Session Eight
25th May 2007

Tina came alone, and, as agreed, we used the session to make a relaxation tape to support Tina between our sessions. I used the help of Henry Leo Bolduc's book, and also Joe Keaney's deepening techniques(both listed in the Bibliography) and adapted all of it to suit Tina's specific needs. I have attended training courses with both of these fine hypnotherapists, and these classes have been of ongoing benefit in my therapeutic work for many years. Specifically, I used "Entering Self-Hypnosis 1" pages 60-61 and "Sexual Fulfillment Cycle" pages 109-111 from Bolduc, and I used the ego reinforcing suggestion on page 19 of Joe Keaney's book as well as the count-up taught on Joe Keaney's courses.* The tape was made live in the session and my own input was thought out beforehand but delivered spontaneously in the moment.

The complete transcript of the tape is in Appendix I at the end of this book.

Making the tape took about 30 minutes, and Tina seemed to relax very well during the session, and she told me that she enjoyed it. I suggested that she would listen to the tape three times per week, and she agreed to do this.

* I am very grateful to both authors for giving me permission to use and reprint their work.

SESSION NINE
31ST MAY 2007

Tina's Journal:

24th May 2007: Read another chapter of my book which was all about having sex. It said "It takes time, effort and a fantastic relationship to learn to give and receive pleasure." Sex is a learned and practised thing—the result of getting to know each other mentally and physically.

31st May 2007: Alice made me a relaxation tape, which I find great. It helps me to relax my whole body and unwind. It gives me positive thoughts about myself and my relationship with Darren, and also lots of positive thoughts towards sex. I try to listen to it every day.

We have spent lots of time hugging and kissing over the past week, making time for ourselves as a couple. We both enjoyed doing this a lot. I let Darren use KY Jelly on me. I still was a bit nervous, but it was a start or a step in the right direction.

Darren's Journal:

Last week, we both went to see Alice together. It was nice for me to get involved again, although I did not mind taking a back seat for the last six or seven weeks. I was very excited to know that it is time for both of us to become more physical and start trying to progress slowly to be more intimate with each other. We used our KY Jelly to give each other a massage. We had a very special evening on Thursday from 5.30p.m. We spent time together on a night off from work, sport, and television. We took Alice's advice and went to bed early. Took a shower each and lay in bed naked. Tina was quite nervous, and, after a while, we began using the gel on each other. I enjoyed Tina's massage of my penis very much. It was very sensual. My massage on Tina did not go as well. Tina was not quite ready just yet. She might try the KY Jelly herself first, until she gets used to putting anything into the vagina. It was Tina's period earlier in the week, so we did not get as much practical homework done as we would have liked. It is Tina's birthday soon, and I intend to do something special for it, as I feel it is a time when Tina needs my full support more than ever. I hope Tina and Alice get on well making the relaxation tape.

OUR MEETING TOGETHER:

We discussed Tina's fear about allowing Darren to put KY Jelly around the entrance to her vagina. Darren, who is by nature very gentle and considerate, reassured Tina that he would not hurt her and would only progress to the extent that she allowed. I acknowledged Darren's care and, simultaneously I emphasised to Tina how vital it was for her to go through some level of discomfort in order to make progress. This was always a fine line for me in this particular therapy. I felt I sometimes needed to be firm with Tina about engaging in the agreed exercises, yet I did not want to create a level of discomfort which might cause her to become disheartened.

As always, I reminded Tina that the obstacles to progress were solely in her mind. I stressed that the vagina is a flexible, elastic organ which can allow the passage of a baby. Therefore a gentle massage with her husband's finger is no problem for that wonderful area of the body. I reassured her that her discomfort is caused by old fear, which has no place in her life now. I also stressed that once she tolerates some discomfort at the initial touching by her husband, she will gradually become more at ease, and I strongly encouraged her to come back next week and tell me she had made some progress.

At this point, I also encouraged Tina to give a little more to Darren, so that their sexual touching could become more of a mutual pleasure giving rather than something Darren was "doing to her." I encouraged her to massage his penis to the point of bringing him to ejaculation, as Tina had never seen Darren ejaculate and had no idea what this was like to experience. I described the semen as a cloudy coloured warm liquid which carries millions of sperm. I invited Tina to reflect on the wonder of this amazing liquid having the power to create life within her and to see it as a friend.

Then I asked the couple to reflect on experiences in their lives which had been very fearful for them. Tina immediately remembered and spoke with great upset about a time as a child of seven in communion class when she was asked to read aloud, and a little boy in the class laughed out loud at her. She was mortified! From that moment to this, she had never again read aloud in public. She was very hurt by the boy, and she released the feelings of the hurt seven-year-old inner child in this session. As we spoke, she could see that he was just a child too and had no idea how much pain he had caused her.

Darren's biggest fear was around basic maths, but he was well able to manage using a calculator. Also, he said he was by nature a quiet person, but had come to accept himself and to allow himself to be in company without having to speak a lot. I believed that it was helpful to Tina that Darren also identified with having some fears. At every stage in the therapy, I reassured Tina that her experiences were shared by many other people.

As always, we concluded the session by bringing golden light into the spaces created by releasing old fears. As a therapist, my hope was that, as Tina released each painful emotion (in this case fear), her mind would be freer to move forward with positive changes in her life.

SESSION TEN
8ᵀᴴ JUNE 2007

TINA'S JOURNAL this week read as follows:

Still listening to my relaxation tape. Darren got me earphones, which makes it easier to listen to it, as I do not worry about anyone hearing it, etc.

Our homework was for Darren to use KY Jelly on me twice this week. I am still nervous, or still anxious more so than nervous.

Found a book at home in Mum's which a friend had given her to read, called "Creating Health." One of the chapters was about "Sexual Inadequacy," so I read it. Great to read that I am not the only one. That there are people out there going through what I am going through. I know Alice has told me this before. But you can never hear it enough.

We spoke last week about how I am nervous about reading or talking out loud in public. When I was in school, I remember being laughed at when I read out loud and made mistakes.

Darren's Journal:

I read in our guide book this week about parents talking to their children about sex and relationships, body changes at puberty etc. There were good points about how to deal with queries from children of different ages; for example young children's questions about why boys are different to girls. The advice to parents is to give the information necessary for the stage the child is at, but, from an early age use proper language for body parts rather than made-up names, and do not go into too much detail of the full biology at a young age. A parent will be able to talk at ease with their teenager, if they had an open relationship with their child from a young age. Talking about sex and relationships will be normal and relaxed for both parent and child if it is ongoing over their childhood. It is important to be a good listener and to let the child make their own decisions, while giving some guidance. Also, self esteem is very important, and it is up to the parent to try and build up their child's self-worth through praise and support.

This week was also a good week for Tina and myself. We had a nice weekend at home for the bank holiday, spending time together, and doing odd jobs in the house and garden. We spent time together and used the KY Jelly on each other. Tina is getting more at ease and used to me inserting my finger into her vagina and moving it around a bit. We are making good progress.

I was thinking about my weaknesses and fears. I am not too worried but am weak at basic maths and use a calculator at work. I have no problem with more advanced maths. I am also quiet in a crowd, but it is not really a problem, as I am not really shy.

OUR MEETING TOGETHER:

In our detailed discussion about the couple's sexual contact this week, and important point arose, which neither one had written in the journal. Tina had in massaged Darren's penis and when she got tired he brought himself to the point of ejaculation with Tina watching him. This was the first Time Tina had ever experienced a man's orgasm or seen semen. Tina started to heave and ran in to the bathroom and actually vomited. When we spoke about the reason for this, Tina was not fully aware of it, but it seemed that perhaps it was a combination of the smell of the semen and even more so the major emotional relief of having experienced something which she had dreaded all her life. As a therapist, I noted the strength of her reaction, and I decided to focus on praising her for having masturbated Darren and witnessed his ejaculation. I reassured her that, like every other part of her sexual growth, this experience too would gradually become more comfortable for her. I therefore urged her to repeat the experience in the coming week to see how she

would feel about it.

Session Eleven
15TH June 2007

Tina's journal read as follows:

Did not do great on the homework end this week. The weekend just went by so fast. Then during the week I got my period, so we did not use the KY Jelly on me. We did not get to spend as much "our time" this week as we would have liked to. Darren started working in a new place, so he was under a bit of pressure and was tired at night. I was also tired maybe due to my period. I did put my finger in Darren's semen. Did not get sick! I was fine about it.

Darren's Journal:

This week I read a chapter about puberty in boys and girls. From a boy's point of view, I could agree with the information given. I found it interesting and learned a lot about puberty in girls and periods, which I would not have had that much knowledge about, other than it happens once a month.

There was a good table about the woman's 28 day cycle, where it goes through the different stages and how the woman is feeling; i.e. days 1-6, 7-13 etc. At different stages, there are hormonal imbalances and going from good form to tiredness and stomach pain. I feel I will look back at this from time to time to try and be aware of what Tina is going through. The chapter also had good diagrams of both male and female reproductive systems.

This week was not quite as good as last, as we did not get to do as much together as we planned. At the weekend, I was busy around the house and getting prepared for a new job. We did get to the beach with relatives on Sunday.

Tina's period came on Tuesday, and she did not feel in the mood for much and could not do our home-work. On Thursday night, she was feeling a bit down from not getting much progress in the week. We concentrated on me, and I masturbated for her, and she looked at and put her finger in the semen. Tina was okay with the semen this week and felt very happy to have some information to report back to Alice. It was also good for me, as Tina is more involved with my masturbation. Before all this, I was a bit frustrated with having to do it all myself, and I missed sex.

I am sure we will make up for this week over the week-end with plenty of special time together.

Our Meeting Together:

In this session, the couple spoke how Darren had mastur-

bated in Tina's presence, and about Tina's willingness to be

with the semen and get used to it. I affirmed her for having

the courage to experience it again this week, having had such

a strong reaction last week. I was pleased with her progress.

However, I also pointed out to the couple how they had al-

lowed other events in the past week to take them away from their sexual relationship. I stated that this was an attitude that needed to change. They had been married for six years and had become used to a relationship without sex. Now it was vital to make regular time for their intimate relationship. I suggested regular sexual contact, about three times per week. I stressed the importance of making this a priority and devoting plenty of time to it. Work or friendships or household duties should not be allowed to take their focus off their loving relationship together. I encouraged them to create a new habit in their marriage of regular sexual contact. I assured them that, in time, this would then become the norm for them.

Then we spoke about the biological facts of reproduction. Having worked with many couples dealing with fertility issues, I am very aware of the monthly cycle, dates when pregnancy is most likely etc. I explained to the couple that research clearly shows that couples who have regular and frequent sexual intercourse; i.e. daily or every second day, are likely to become pregnant within twelve months. Also, sex on certain days in the cycle is most likely to result in pregnancy. In an average 28 day cycle, days 8-13 are often most fertile. This is because the sperm can live for several days in the fertile mucus of the vagina just before ovulation, while the woman's egg lives only about twenty four hours after being released. Since it is not easy to pinpoint the exact moment of ovulation, the chances of pregnancy are greatest when a couple have sex in the days immediately preceding ovulation. Also, because of the thin mucus in the vagina on these days, sex is often most enjoyable.

Though the couple were not at the stage of having the possibility of pregnancy at this stage in the therapy, they were very interested in speaking about all this and learning about it. One of their biggest motivators for coming to therapy was their desire to have children and their awareness that at over thirty five, the time had come to take action on this. By discussing with them the facts of reproduction, I wanted to give them hope and to keep them motivated to do their sexual homework every week.

SESSION TWELVE
22ND JUNE 2007

Tina's Journal:

*I listened to my relaxation tape every day this week.
Did not miss a day. So I am very happy with that.
Darren and I went to Saturday night mass and had
the whole of Sunday morning to be together. It was
lovely. Darren used KY Jelly on me. I was still a bit
nervous but better than before.*

*Last week, Alice spoke to us about periods etc. They
happen every 28 days, and around ten days after your
period you have a better chance of becoming pregnant. I read a chapter about first time sex. It said that
for a couple who have known each other for some
time in a long term relationship first-time sex is just a
milestone on their sexual journey together.*

Darren's Journal:

*This week, I read a chapter about love and relation-
ships. It is important to teach teenagers to stand up
for themselves and not have sex until they are ready.
Love can be shown in ways other than sex. First time
sex takes time to get used to. It can be embarrassing,
it can hurt, and it takes time to be good at it. As long
as it is between two consenting adults, sex is as natural and as normal as breathing.*

*This week was a much better week for Tina and me.
We spent much more time together. We lay in bed*

Sunday morning. I gave Tina a massage with my finger and put it into her vagina. She was quite relaxed once I put in my finger. On Thursday night, we went to bed early and enjoyed more time together. After being a bit nervous to start, Tina relaxed using the breathing exercises, and I left my finger in her vagina for 20 minutes to a half an hour, moving it around and in and out. We did not get to concentrate much on me this week, but we are both very happy. I think we are progressing well.

OUR MEETING TOGETHER:

I was pleased with the progress the couple had made this week. Tina was allowing prolonged penetration of the vagina now, and even though she was still somewhat anxious at the moment of penetration, she was using her breathing and pelvic tilts to help her. The couple were following my suggested guidelines and feeling really good about their progress. I spoke with them about making the current activity a more loving and mutual act. I encouraged them to really allow their bodies to enjoy the touching. I believed that this would happen naturally in time, but I also wished them to focus on it. I also suggested that Tina pay a bit more attention to Darren's needs, as I noticed that he was always very attentive to her, whereas her anxiety had caused her to be very self-focused.

I asked the couple whether they feel ready to move to the next stage of intimate touching. They were about to go on a short holiday and would have two weeks before I saw them again, so they were enthusiastic about moving forward. I suggested to them that they continue the mutual touching with hands using KY Jelly and that Darren continue to penetrate Tina's vagina with his finger. In addition, I suggested they now move to the point where having completed the foreplay, Darren would lie on top of Tina and rub his penis into her external genitalia. I asked them at this point not to attempt penetration with the penis but to get comfortable with the position first. Of course I wanted them to note how this went for them and come back and speak with me about it.

SESSION THIRTEEN
5ᵀᴴ JULY 2007

Tina's Journal:

We had a great time on holidays, but I was unable to listen to my tape for four days, which I missed. We talked last week with Alice about how we have been living our lives without sex in it for so long. We have to learn to make time for it in our lives now. We also spoke about pregnancy—something I had given up on. I had closed off all my thoughts about having a baby etc. It was like I had switched off my biological clock. I still find it hard to believe it can be possible for us to have a baby, please God. I suppose I am getting my biological clock repaired, and this clock is worth repairing. I read another chapter in my book Let's Talk Sex. I took this out of it: "It has been said that a good relationship can sustain an indifferent sex life, but that a good sex life will never maintain a poor relationship."

Darren's Journal:

The last fortnight went well. The first Sunday we spent together and stayed on in bed Sunday morning. We used the KY Jelly on each other at the same time, making it a more loving act rather than just a procedure. It went well, and I also lay on top of Tina in "the man on top" position, rubbing against Tina. Tina was happy with this, and I also enjoyed it. We went abroad on Thursday and really enjoyed the

*weekend, swimming, cycling, and horse riding. We re-
ally enjoyed our time together and with our friends.*

*We were quite tired after the weekend, and it was
hard to get back into our exercises. Tina found it a bit
harder to get back to it after a bit of a break and not
listening to her tape over the weekend and not talking
to Alice. Wednesday morning, we used the KY Jelly.
Tina rubbed me, and I rubbed her. After Tina had
an orgasm, she just wanted to be hugged and did not
want me to insert my finger into her vagina. I finished
off my own orgasm.*

*Thursday morning, we tried again. It went very well.
I used my finger, and it just seemed to gradually go
into the vagina, unknown to Tina and myself, after
Tina initially being a bit anxious. We also tried "the
man on top" position again. It went well, and we
both enjoyed just rubbing against each other. Overall,
we had a very good fortnight but did not do as many
exercises as we wanted. We know we have to keep
up plenty of these exercises, as we are seeing that the
more we do, the easier it gets. It also becomes enjoyable for both of us. We are both very happy at the
moment.*

OUR MEETING TOGETHER:

The couple were now making very real and tangible progress,

and we were all pleased. We shared our joy as we spoke in

the session. I was aware that Darren always listened atten-

tively and was absolutely committed to following my suggestions. He was also recording the couple's progress in exact detail. For Tina, the challenges were greater, but Darren's commitment was a vital strength and support to her. In an effort to give Tina another psychological aid for the next stages of therapy, I decided to write an affirmation for her.

An affirmation is a positive self-statement, and, when repeated often, it penetrates the subconscious mind which comes to believe the statement and bring it into reality. The wording of affirmations is vital, as they need to be always framed positively and in the present tense. I often write affirmations for my clients to support them in achieving their goals in therapy and in their lives. At this session, I explained affirmations to Tina and Darren, and then I composed one on a piece of paper and handed it to Tina. I asked her to read it out loud three times for us. I asked her how it sounded to her, and she said she was comfortable with it. I then requested that she write it into her journal, and, as part of her homework for next week, change words or add to it as she thought appropriate for her. I also explained that repetition is the key to successfully bringing about the facts stated in the affirmation, so I asked her to repeat it morning and evening and several times during the day. This is what I wrote for her:

"I am a beautiful sexual woman, and I enjoy a comfortable and loving and regular sexual relationship with my husband."

Darren said he would like an affirmation too and asked me if I would compose one for him. This is what I wrote and he transcribed it into his journal:

"I am a kind, loving, and sexually affectionate husband."

Darren's affirmation expressed the truth of what was happening already, whereas Tina's spoke in the present tense about what we all hoped would become reality. The subconscious mind does not distinguish, and so what is affirmed in the present as fact becomes a reality.

As the couple were now moving nearer to the point of having sexual intercourse, I believed it was important for Tina to consciously choose to engage in deeper sexual contact, and so I also gave her a homework assignment of writing into her journal the reasons she wanted to have sex with Darren. I asked her to write not phrases but full sentences beginning with "I."

SESSION FOURTEEN
12TH JULY 2007

Tina's Journal:

This week, we talked about affirmations or positive self-statements. Alice gave me one to say a few times a day: "I am a beautiful, sexual woman, and I enjoy a comfortable and loving and regular sexual relationship with my husband." I was to make up my own affirmation, but I like Alice's one. However, I did add one word to it; i.e. "confident." "I am a beautiful, confident, sexual woman." I find it a great help the more I say it out loud or in my head. I think children should be taught about affirmations in school, for example each child given one special affirmation for them to say each day. What a great start in life that would be for them. My homework this week was to write the reasons I want to have sex with Darren; a) because I love him; b) I want to be a real woman; c) to have a child; d) to be normal. I would like to escape this dark place and to put my past thoughts about sex away for good. And this is what I am doing with the help of Darren and Alice. I am going to a much brighter place.

Darren's Journal:

*I finished the book **Let's Talk Sex**. I found it good and informative, and we will keep it as a reference when we need information. Hopefully, we will need it to advise our own children in the future!! We had a good week with both of us feeling very positive towards the idea of having sex so near. We spent Sunday* *morning together and used the KY Jelly. Also, Tina let me try the "man on top" position rubbing against her. We also did the same on Monday morning as we were conscious that her period was due any day. Tina is talking very positive about next week and trying to place the penis in the vagina. I am taking the weekend off to have some special time together over the weekend.*

OUR MEETING TOGETHER:

At this point in the therapy, I was pleased with the progress the couple were making. They could now talk with me about their sexual behaviour with reasonable comfort and with the language to describe what was happening. Tina was able to allow penetration of the vagina with Darren's finger and relax as he moved his finger around inside of her. She was also at ease with Darren lying on top of her and rubbing his penis against her external genitalia. It was clear to me that the couple themselves were now hopeful and could even see a point where they would be having full sexual intercourse. They were pushing themselves to make progress, and I was simply supporting them.

I expressed my admiration for the progress the couple were making. I pointed out to Tina that she has already allowed penetration of the vagina with the speculum during the smear test which is a metal object the same size as an erect penis but not nearly as pleasant to feel. I therefore asserted that she could soon decide to allow penetration of the penis. I reassured the couple that initially it would be great if they could just be able to insert the penis even a small distance inside the entrance to the vagina. Then they could gradually get comfortable with that and insert it further and move it around and eventually get to the point where Darren could have an orgasm in the vagina.

One of the nice things that had happened at this stage was that the couple were using their trips to see me as a little outing that they could enjoy. On the long summer evenings, they were driving an hour and a half to see me. I live and work in the beautiful seaside region of Curracloe, County Wexford, and after our session, the couple would visit the beach, have a walk, and Darren would go for a swim. Then they would have something to eat and take their time going

home.

SESSION FIFTEEN
20TH JULY 2007

Tina's Journal:

Reason's why I want to have sex with Darren: 1. Because I love him so much. 2. Because I want to feel like a real woman. 3. Because I want to have a child with Darren. 4. I want to be normal like everyone else.

The homework for this week didn't get done! i.e. have sex with Darren. But I am still very pleased with myself at the great effort and progress we have made over this week. We took Sunday as a totally "us" day. Just the two of us for Sunday dinner. It was fab, good food and a bottle of wine. We both really enjoyed it. Very romantic! But it just didn't happen. But we have been trying every night except Tuesday night. I think it is going well and moving forward. We never spent that much time trying before and also enjoying it and becoming more relaxed with one another. I feel very positive about it all which is a welcome change, and Darren has been so good about it all and loving to me. And I know that I will write in this diary soon that I had sex with my husband Darren.

Darren's Journal:

This week also went very well. We had a nice day together on Saturday. On Sunday we had cooked dinner for the two of us, whereas often we invite family members for Sunday dinner. We made it special by using the dining room. We had some wine, and the plan was to go to bed after dinner. We did go to bed, but we were both a bit uptight. We were not in the right frame of mind. The day was very special.

On Monday night, we tried again, and it went well. But we did not get to put in the penis. We also tried on Wednesday and Thursday nights. It went better on Thursday night with us getting the head of the penis to the first part of the vagina. Tina was very relaxed for me inserting my finger but was not quite ready for the full penis. We are very happy with the progress and trying so regularly. Tina is at the right stage of her cycle for sex, and I feel we will make progress to-night or tomorrow. Tina is also very positive.

OUR MEETING TOGETHER:

At this point, about four months into the therapy, I was pleased with the progress the couple had made. They were spending considerably more intimate time together than when I first met them, they were engaging in ever deepening levels of sexual touching, and they were both very hopeful about soon having full sexual intercourse. They were both able to speak more openly and freely about their bodies and their sexuality. Tina now felt reasonably comfortable with mutual touching of the genitals, Darren inserting his finger into her vagina and moving it around for periods as long as twenty minutes, and Darren lying on top of her and rubbing his penis against her external genitalia.

While acknowledging their successes, I was also a little concerned that rather than enjoying their progress and staying with the stage they had achieved, they were both pushing forward toward full sexual intercourse. I spoke with the couple about this. Also, I pointed out to Tina that there were a lot of references to "trying" in her journal. Using the word "try" can set a client up for failure, so I suggested they enjoy the sexual behaviours they were currently engaged in and gently move forward when ready. The next step was simply to place the head of the penis inside the entrance to the vagina and experience that even briefly. The couple had done this once in the past week.

Again, I reassured Tina that there would be some discomfort as the tip of the penis entered her vagina, but I affirmed that she would be able to tolerate that and subsequently feel great about her progress. Darren stressed to Tina that he would never hurt her and would always listen to her needs and stop at any point if she wished to do so. While it was obviously vital that Tina would never feel "forced" to do anything, I spoke with Darren about being encouraging and not giving in too easily to Tina's fear. This was an important balancing point in the therapy. Tina needed to tolerate some discomfort in order to make progress. However, the discomfort needed to be at a level which would not distress or dishearten her. Darren was by nature very gentle and loving, and so he was always sensitive to Tina's needs. Tina knew that she was very blessed to have such a good partner.

Session Sixteen
26ᵀᴴ July 2007

Tina's Journal:

Have not achieved sex yet! But working hard to be successful. We are closer to achieving it this week than last week. So that's a move forward to our goal. I know the more we try, the closer to doing it we will be.

I know it is hard on Darren at times putting up with me. But he has been so good and kind. And so patient.

I read back on my diary today. I have been going to Alice for four months now. I read my achievements so far which have been good. Also my low points and my fears, but I have overcome most of them now.

Darren's Journal:

Did not get to do homework this week. This week was also a good week. We made time for intimacy over the weekend.

Our Meeting Together:

Darren had been working at a distance from home this week,

and therefore did not have time to write his journal prior

to our session. However, he described the sexual contact of the couple as having been good and enjoyable. He had placed the tip of his penis inside Tina's vagina on a couple of occasions, and though she was not relaxed, both parties felt good about the progress. I affirmed that they were doing well and simply encouraged them to aim to get the penis in a little further and for a little longer in the week ahead, and I assured Tina that she would gradually get more relaxed as she got used to this experience. Just four months ago, the couple could not even have imagined having the level of sexual intimacy they have now achieved.

I liked Tina's idea to read back over her journal. It contained tangible evidence for her of how far she had come in just four months. In this phase where the couple had hit a plateau in which progress was less obvious, the journal was an encouragement and support to Tina to keep up the exercises and exploration of self.

In an effort to take some pressure off the couple regarding their sexual relationship, I suggested that we use some of this therapy session to focus on how they gave and received love and support in other ways in their marriage. Though it was obvious to me that this couple had a very strong relationship apart from the sexual problems, they had never actually verbalised with me what made them happy to be together. It was lovely to listen to them express their appreciation for one another.

Tina said that Darren was her best friend. He was affectionate and understanding no matter what her mood. They shared many interests, such as walking in nature and other outdoor sports and leisure activities. Darren had become friendly with Tina's friends and their husbands, so the couple had some regular contact with other couples, which was mutually enjoyable for them. Also, Tina was very grateful to Darren for his support of her parents who regularly visited. Tina said that Darren was a fun person to be with, and they enjoyed regular holidays and day trips. Neither person liked going to pubs and seldom drank alcohol, apart

from an occasional glass of wine with dinner on special occasions. Their home was a welcoming, peaceful place.

Darren said that Tina was a loving and good wife. He
particularly appreciated the effort Tina made to create a
warm home. She was a reasonably good housekeeper but
put people first. She was very supportive in cooking him
good food and making healthy home-made soup for his
lunches at work. Darren also expressed appreciation for Tina's playfulness and good humour. I had seen and enjoyed
this quality of Tina's in our sessions together. Of the three
of us, Tina was the most light-hearted, and could sometimes
bring a laugh to the sessions when the work was serious.
Often, she herself was the target of the humour, though in
a nice way.

SESSION SEVENTEEN
3ʳᴰ AUGUST 2007

Tina's Journal:

I am a beautiful sexual woman and I enjoy a comfortable and loving regular sexual relationship with my husband.

Sometimes I can't believe that I am just right at the door of having sex. This thing that I have feared so much over the past few years, that has upset my life for so many years will soon be over. It is so hard to imagine not having this problem anymore. I don't know how I let it build up to be such a problem in my life. It is like having a bad dream and I have awakened from it at last. I have to pinch myself sometimes to see if it is true. I am very happy with myself. And I look forward to my new life with sex in it so much. It's like a dream come true.

Darren's Journal:

This week was another good week for Tina and me. Over the weekend, we made time for sex twice. We took things slowly, just gently placing the penis in Tina. I got to move it around a little. We were hoping to do a good bit of practising during the week, but Tina's period came on Tuesday morning. We still got to spend time kissing and hugging. We are looking forward to the long weekend and having a bit of quality time together.

Our Meeting Together:

I acknowledged Tina's feelings as expressed in her journal. On the one hand, she was thrilled with her progress, almost to the point of not believing it was happening to her. She now believed without doubt that she would soon have sex with her husband. On the other hand, I also picked up the underlying sadness of having waited six years of her marriage to address her sexual problems. I said that I too felt sad for her that she had suffered so long in silence and isolation. I felt sad for her giving up on her dreams of having children. I affirmed that she deserved to have a good sexual relationship and she deserved to have children simply because she was a human being, and a very beautiful and good human being. With that Tina began to cry and told me that she had felt in the past that she did not deserve anything good to happen to her.

I encouraged her to release her feelings of sadness for what she had done to herself over the years. As always, I affirmed that releasing the emotional pain would make room for healing. I explained to her that when she cut off her connection to her own body and her sexuality, she had also cut off so many emotions including her love of children and desire to have her own babies. I invited her to let herself dream now of being pregnant and having her own baby. I told her that I thought she would be a wonderful mother and that a child would be very fortunate to have parents like herself and Darren. Tina was very emotional and cried a lot in this session. She seemed deeply touched by my kind and supportive comments.

Session Eighteen
17th August 2007

This time we had a two week interval between our sessions, as Tina had been ill.

Tina's Journal:

I am a beautiful sexual woman, and I enjoy a comfortable and loving regular sexual relationship with my husband.

I was ill for the first week, so we were not able to be sexual together. But we got to spend time together, even though I was not the best of company at times.

Alice said last week that I have put all my feelings into a box. All my thoughts about having children I have locked away in this box. I felt I did not deserve the right to be a mother. I never fuss over children much, as it would only remind me of what I could not have. It was very hard to see my friends all having children. I would be delighted for them, but a part of me would get a bit upset when I heard one of them was expecting. Now it is time to take out "the box," which I have done. Next step is to open it! And let me dream a little about having children.

Alice said something last week that totally summed up exactly how I felt about myself for years. That I thought I did not <u>deserve</u> to be happy.

Darren's Journal:

*Things did not go quite as planned for the first week.
We both had the weekend off, but Tina was ill with
aches and pains all over. She was a bit frustrated
that we could not do anything as we had such plans.
We knew it was just a matter of waiting a few days.
We did get to spend a lot of time together, just not
sexually.*

*We had a better week this week. Tina still was a bit ill
with a bad cold, but we tried to do our best. Sunday
night, we had a bit of intimate time. I put in my finger
and rubbed my penis against Tina's vagina, and we
both moved like during sex. This was nice for us. On
Tuesday night, we tried again. We were both under a
bit of pressure. I put in my finger and tried to put in
my penis, but it was just not happening for us. Tina
had a lot of work pressure over the weekend. On
Thursday night, we had plans for more sex, but we
talked instead, as Tina had some things on her mind
which were upsetting her. I think she wants to talk to
Alice about them. Tina talked a little to me, but I feel
she has a lot more to tell Alice. We did spend a lot of
loving time together. Next week will not be as hectic
as this one, and I am sure we will do much better.*

OUR MEETING TOGETHER:

I recognised at the end of the last session that Tina had

been deeply touched by my statement that she deserved to

be happy. However, I had no idea of the impact that statement had on her, and I was totally surprised by what came up for healing in this session. In my estimation, the issue dealt with in this session and the next one was one of the core issues which had contributed to Tina's shutting down of her sexuality.

This is the essence of the story as Tina told it to me in this session. It was the first time in our therapy that this major issue from Tina's life had been mentioned by either herself or her husband. Tina began by saying that her feeling of not deserving happiness went a long way back in her life to her very first romantic relationship. She explained to me that her first boyfriend had taken his own life, and she had been deeply upset by it. She was crying and her husband offered to leave the room so she could speak with me alone. Tina wanted him to leave, and I too felt it appropriate as it would give her space to express feelings about this previous relationship which might be uncomfortable for her husband to hear.

After her leaving certificate at eighteen years of age, Tina had gone away to college and was living in college accommodation. In the first year, she met and fell in love with a young man in the same year. They had a very fun and light-hearted and romantic relationship for several months. The couple spent a lot of their free time together and went on long walks in the countryside. Though they were affectionate in kissing and hugging, they both understood that they were not ready for a sexual relationship. When the summer holidays arrived, the couple parted and went home to their families for the summer holidays. They lived about fifty miles apart, and since Tina did not drive, Paddy used to drive to see her as often as he could at weekends. After a few weeks, Tina found the relationship a strain and felt concerned at the effort Paddy was making to maintain it. She told him she wanted a break from the relationship. He was upset, but said he understood. They spoke on the phone a couple of times over the next few weeks, and then one weekend Tina got a call to say that Paddy had taken his own life.

She was very upset and went to the funeral with a friend. She met Paddy's family to whom she had been introduced during their dating. They spoke and comforted one another and his family seemed fine with her.

However, Tina told me that she had blamed herself for Paddy's suicide. She thought that she had hurt him a lot by ending the relationship. Also she felt he would not have done it had he been able to look forward to seeing her each week. She believed she had no right to be happy, since she had deeply hurt someone she loved. I explained to her that one of the awful legacies of every suicide is the pain that loved ones feel in relation to unanswered questions about why the person would chose to die.

Tina and I discussed her beliefs about the suicide, and I challenged some of her assumptions. I acknowledged that the break-up of their relationship may have played some part in Paddy's decision to take his own life. She would never know the extent of the part it played. However, I said I doubted it was the full cause. After all, they were a young couple, and it was normal at their stage to have relationships which might be on and off. Also there had been an interval of several weeks between the breakup and his death.

Whatever the hurt she had caused Paddy, I explained to her that it was pointless for her to continue punishing herself. Paddy was now in the spiritual world and would be getting a lot of help to heal his life and learn from his experiences. He would not want Tina to punish herself and hold back on her own life because of what he had done. Paddy was dead, his life had ended almost twenty years ago, but Tina had her own life to live, and it was vital that she lived it to the full.

I felt it was very important to guide Tina through the process of healing her guilt about Paddy. She needed to ask for his forgiveness for the hurt she caused him, and she needed to trust that she would receive that forgiveness. Most of all, she needed to forgive herself and let go of any emotional attachment to Paddy which may have been holding her back in her own life. I lent Tina a copy of a book called "Embraced by the Light" by Betty J. Eadie, which is a very encouraging picture of what happens after death, and which I regularly use as a resource in bereavement counselling. As homework, I asked Tina to write a letter to Paddy, saying everything she would like to say to him, including her regrets, appreciation, sadness, and asking for his forgiveness for any hurt she caused him. I explained that, in the next session, she would read this letter aloud to me, and then we would burn it together. When this was completed, if she wished, I could carry out a Reiki healing session to help her let go of Paddy. Tina was very open to accepting any help I could offer, so we called her husband into the room and explained to him that Tina needed to attend alone for the next session. As always, Darren was very supportive and accommodating.

As I reflected on this session when the couple had left, I was both surprised and very pleased that this deep issue from Tina's life had come to light. Tina had told me during the session that she had previously not thought to share it because she had not seen it as relevant to her sexual problems. I saw it as one of the core experiences which caused her to cut off her sexuality. My interpretation was that Tina internalised her guilt about causing the death of her first boyfriend and subconsciously punished herself by never fully giving herself to a man. Also she may have feared that letting a man get very close to her would be dangerous for both him and her. She may also have unconsciously been punishing every subsequent man in her life for the hurt caused by Paddy. The mind is deep and fascinating, and truthfully, I am still not sure which explanation, if any of the above, was the most accurate in Tina's case.

The issue of Paddy's suicide came up for healing as Tina was nearing the stage of allowing full penetration of the vagina by her husband's penis. Tina was ill for the week before this therapy session. It was as if the cells of her body, particularly her sexual organs may have been holding this trauma, which could no longer be suppressed as she got closer to herself as a woman and also closer to having sex with her husband. Since Tina had released so much emotion in this session and was willing to engage in some healing exercises, I felt confident that she would be able to overcome this block. Years of suppressed pain once brought to light can often be healed very quickly.

SESSION NINETEEN
23ᴿᴰ AUGUST 2007

Tina's Journal:

I had a very emotional week. I talked to Alice about Paddy. It was the first time I really talked to anyone about Paddy. And how I felt about his passing away and the way he has affected me over the years. I felt so good after talking about it to Alice. Like it was a new start for me!

She gave me a book to read called "Embraced by the Light" by Betty J. Eadie. I found this book so good. I felt so good every time I read a chapter. I just wanted to read and read. These are little notes I took out of it. "Light, truth and love. Darkness does not await us at the end of life, but rather loving light." It said that death was actually a "rebirth." Also the grave was never intended for the spirit—only for the body. We can alter or redirect our life at any time. We must love ourselves. Forgive myself and then move forward. If I had hurt someone, seek their forgiveness. I could begin to heal myself spiritually first, then emotionally, mentally, and physically.

OUR MEETING TOGETHER:

In this session, once I had checked with Tina how she was and read her journal, we got right down to work, as we had a lot to cover. Firstly Tina read aloud to me the letter she wrote to Paddy. I suggested that she read it slowly, so that she could really feel what she was saying. The letter was warm and heartfelt and expressed everything she had appreciated and loved about him. Also, it expressed her deep sorrow at his death and explained how she had blamed herself. Finally, it affirmed her need to move forward and her hope that he was at peace and would forgive her for any hurt she had caused. It ended by saying she hoped that someday they would meet again. Tina cried a lot as she read the letter, and I complimented her on her very sincere and honest effort at putting her feelings into words. I said I believed that Paddy's spirit heard her words, and that he would be happy for her. We agreed to put the letter aside and go outside and burn it at the end of our session.

Then we moved on to complete the Reiki healing session for cutting the ties that bind people. I have been a Reiki master and teacher for over ten years and sometimes when I feel it will be of benefit to a client, I incorporate elements of

Reiki healing into my psychotherapy work. I explained to Tina that when two people have a deep connection, there are energetic bonds that link the two people at various points in the body, for example, there might be a bond linking one's heart to the other, or one's head to the other, or even one's private parts to the other. The Reiki healing session is very spiritual, and cuts only the bonds which are no longer helpful to the two people. In other words, it ends any negative psychic or emotional ties between the two individuals. I affirmed that in doing this healing session, Tina and I were wishing everything good for Paddy and hoping that he too would benefit from the healing.

Then we proceeded with the session. I asked Tina to sit comfortably in her chair with her eyes closed. I invited her to ask for protection from her guardian angels and guides. Then I went through the procedure for cutting the ties, using Reiki healing symbols and prayers. The words used are beautiful and repetitive and have a hypnotic quality, which is comforting to the listener. The process took about twenty minutes. At the end of it, Tina was very relaxed and positive, and she said she felt freer in herself.

Then we walked into the garden, bringing Tina's letter to Paddy, some matches and a tea light, and Tina burned the letter with my help and support. We had some fun doing this as there was a slight wind and we had to light the piece of paper several times. I believe that burning is a powerful process for letting go, where the client sees the past in ashes and can leave it blow away in the wind. That evening, Tina left the garden in good form ready to drive home, and I went back to my therapy room to meet my next client.

Session Twenty
30th August 2007

Tina's Journal:

I feel so content or happy in myself from last week's visit to Alice. I got great relief from the Reiki. It felt like I was getting physical help, as if physically the chains and ropes were being cut between Paddy and I. Which was a great feeling of freedom or relief from my past. The burning of the letter I wrote to Paddy was also a great feeling of relief. The saying of good bye "until we meet again." It all feels like I have sorted out my past, something that has been with me for a few years, the feeling of guilt and torment.

Now it is time to move on and look forward to what the future has in store for me! And enjoy life. No room for regrets. Just positive thinking about life etc. And to treasure my time with Darren, my wonderful husband, my best friend, and my lover.

Darren's Journal:

We had another good week. We are both looking forward to our holidays next week.

On Sunday morning, we did our usual morning in bed. We got to put the penis in and moved around a bit. Not too far in just the head of the penis. Tuesday night, we tried again, but I just put my finger into Tina's vagina. Thursday morning, we tried again, and we got in the penis again, much the same as on

*Sunday. It seems a bit harder to do, as we think it is
time for Tina's period.*

OUR MEETING TOGETHER:

The couple were pleased with their progress and were main-

taining the level of sexual intimacy they had achieved to

date. Having come from a situation of no sexual intimacy,

they were now having sexual play about three times per

week, and they are both enjoying it. While I was pleased

for them, I was also aware that there was still more progress

needed in two stages: (a) Darren to insert his penis fully

into the vagina and (b) full intercourse with ejaculation. I

encouraged them at this session to move to the stage of full

insertion of the penis for several minutes. The couple were

going abroad on holidays for two weeks after this session,

and so it would be three weeks before I saw them again. I

suggested that they take plenty of time for relaxation and

sexual play during the holiday and that Tina use all her ac-

quired resources, e.g. breathing and pelvic tilting to help her to relax sufficiently to allow Darren to insert his penis more deeply into the vagina. I encouraged Tina to continue using her affirmation and relaxation tape while on holiday. Most of all, I wished them a happy holiday in which they would celebrate the great progress they had made on their sexual relationship.

THE THERAPIST'S MIND

IN ORDER TO WRITE THIS BOOK HONESTLY, I need to include a chapter on the effects of the therapy on myself as the therapist. By now, it will be obvious to the reader, that I had a deep connection and a very good working relationship with Tina and Darren. In contrast to other therapies, where I might simply listen and support, due to the nature of the issue, I was a very active participant in all stages of the process.

I was aware at this stage that I was feeling anxious that the couple seemed to be "stuck" in this phase of the process, and it is interesting to me that I am feeling that anxiety now as I write about this. The feeling was very deep and strong. The couple had moved swiftly through the following steps a) touching one another intimately b) applying KY Jelly to the penis and inside the vagina c) Darren inserting his index finger into the vagina and moving it around and in and out gently to open and relax the vagina d) Darren stimulating himself to near orgasm and then inserting the penis into the vagina. For about four weeks now, the couple had been at the same point in which Tina was allowing the penis entry to the opening of the vagina but not allowing any deeper penetration. I believed Tina was unconsciously still keeping control, and I believed it was important not to allow this "stuckness" to continue. After all, this couple had waited almost six years to address their sexual difficulties. They were now both very happy with their progress, and while I was happy too, I knew that they needed to continue to move forward toward their goal of full sexual intercourse with ejaculation. I did not confront this issue with them before their holiday, as I wanted them to have a relaxing time, free from worry. This meant that I held my feelings of anxiety, inadequacy, and lack of sureness about the next step for the holiday weeks. In psychological circles, we use the word "transference" to express unconscious feelings in the client which are picked up and held by the therapist.

I shared about my work with the couple and the effects on me of the current phase of therapy in my own supervision meeting during the holiday period. It felt good to express my doubts and fears about being able to help the couple achieve their final goal. What if I had helped them this far, only to be stuck and unable to progress? Would there be a need to refer them to someone with a different type of expertise? My supervisor was supportive and encouraging, and expressed her belief that I needed to trust my own guidance and trust the therapy process to move forward at the right pace. Maybe I was being impatient? Maybe at some level, I was disappointed that having initially said the couple might be able to have sex by the time of their holidays, this was not happening. In reality, the therapy had progressed very efficiently, and the couple were very pleased with their progress. The supervisor encouraged me to be aware of my own feelings and use them as a guide when working with the couple. I knew my feelings were important, and I decided to bring them into the next session with the couple, still unsure of how I would do this. I was grateful for the support and reassurance of my supervisor.

Session Twenty One
21st September 2007

Before the session, I prayed for guidance to do what was needed. The couple came in looking relaxed and tanned after their holiday. I began by reading the journals.

Tina's Journal:

> We had a wonderful holiday. It was great to spend all day together. It built up a real closeness to one another. It was just what the doctor ordered! I enjoyed it so much. I didn't want to come home, which was a real first for me, as I always want to go home. I was very content on holidays, maybe because we have made progress in our sexual lives. Not like other holidays, hoping that something would happen sexually. But this holiday we were making things happen in our sexual lives.

> We enjoyed the trip to Our Lady's Shrine. We were only there for four hours which was quite short for such a beautiful place. But we prayed to Our Lady, asking her to help us, and we know she will answer our prayers.

> Darren and I have been trying a lot over the holiday and the past week. Some days we find it easy, and other days it's a bit harder. But we are working well together. There is a lot of love between us. So we can have full sex soon.

Darren's Journal:

The last two weeks went very well for us. Tina's period finished just before our holidays, which was great for both swimming and sex. We both enjoyed the holidays and did a good bit of trying to have sex. About four times, I got to put the penis into the vagina. Once Tina was quite relaxed, and I got to move the penis around a good bit. The rest of the time Tina was more nervous. It is no problem for me to put in my finger now, but when it comes to the penis, sometimes I find it quite hard to guide it in. We are now having more fun in bed. We are happy with progress. We are coming along slowly.

OUR MEETING TOGETHER:

The couple shared their delight at having been sexually intimate for the first time ever while on holiday. I acknowledged their feelings, and said I was so pleased for them. Then I spoke about the importance of continuing to move forward toward their ultimate goal, and I asked them to speak about what was happening in the current phase. As always, Darren clearly stated that while Tina was more relaxed at all phases of their intimacy, she was still anxious when he was inserting his penis. When he sensed this discomfort, he stopped. I then asked Tina to speak about what was happening for her. She said she did not know. I said it was important to explore what was happening and that this might be enough to help her move forward. However, if she continued to find this stage particularly difficult, I thought she could ask her G.P. for a small amount of valium to relax her muscles to make the first couple of experiences of the penis entering the vagina more comfortable for her. I am conservative in my attitude to medication in that I believe it has very appropriate uses and can also be over used. Since her G.P had initially referred her to me, I felt in this case, the G.P might be agreeable to give Tina a small amount of medication if we thought it would help.

I then asked Tina if she would be willing to close her eyes and have a conversation with me about what was currently happening for her sexually. She agreed. As she closed her eyes, Darren immediately asked her if she would like him to leave the room. As always, she said "Yes."

The following conversation was very intuitive on my part, and while I remember the main points of it, I have no exact recall for most of it. I too closed my eyes, and I spoke from some deeper part of myself. I explained to Tina that I was speaking as the part of her that wanted to move forward in her sexual relationship with Darren. I asked her to speak as the part of Tina that was stopping her from moving forward. It was really easy for me to be authentic in my part, because I was simply expressing the feelings I had been holding for the past couple of weeks. This is the gist of the conversation:

Alice: Part of Tina that is holding back the sexual relationship, I am the part of you that wants to move forward, and I would like us to discuss what is happening. Are you willing to speak to me?

Tina: Yes, I am.

Alice: Part that is now holding back, I am pleased with your progress to date. Let me say well done on how far you have moved! I am proud of you.

Tina: Thank you. I am proud of myself.

Alice: Part that is now holding back, I also feel that I want to continue moving forward. I want Tina to have full and enjoyable sexual intercourse with her husband, but you are stopping this. I feel frustrated that you are holding me back from going forward. We have come so far, but for four weeks now, you have halted our progress. I would like to understand why you are holding me back, so that I can help you.

Tina: I do not know why I am holding back.

Alice: I believe that you do know, and I would like to understand, so that I can help you.

Tina: I am afraid. My fear is holding me back.

Alice: I acknowledge your fear. Your fear has been with us for all parts of this journey. I am okay with your fear. Part that is holding back, I would like us to go forward together. It is okay to bring your fear, but it is not okay to let your fear stop us from going where we want to go. Could you come forward with me and befriend your fear. Your fear can come with us.

Tina: You are right. I have been allowing my fear to dictate what I do. I will try to go forward in spite of my fear.

Alice: The fear is okay. It is part of you. Just love that part of yourself and still do what you want to do.

Tina: I would like to do that. I would like to move forward and not let my fear stop me.

Alice: I will help you. You can feel your fear and still have full sexual intercourse with Darren. Your fear does not need to be in charge. You can be in charge of your fear. Gradually your fear will lessen, and then you will feel so good about yourself. I will be with you, helping you all the way.

Tina: Thank you. I will do my best.

Session continues:

The trance conversation may have lasted about twenty minutes. I had seen somewhat similar conversations performed by therapists doing psychodrama and also by hypnotherapists for instance speaking to the part of a client that wanted to continue smoking. In my work as a therapist, I am often surprised at the previous learnings which come up for me to use when I feel challenged.

Before the end of the session, Tina and I summarised the conversation we had had, and she said she would move to the next stage of allowing full entry to the penis. I reassured

her that, while there would be some discomfort, she could

do it and would gradually get to like it. I lent Tina my copy

of the book "Feel the Fear and Do it Anyway." I felt that

even the title of the book expressed exactly the position in

which Tina currently found herself.

Then we invited Darren back into the room, and I asked

Tina to explain to him what had transpired. I suggested to

Darren that he encourage Tina to allow full penetration by

the penis this week. I wished the couple well.

Session Twenty Two
28TH September

Tina's Journal:

This week I had a chat with Alice about why Darren and I are not getting anyway further. That we had come to a standstill in our sexual relationship. We were not going backwards, but we were not moving forward.

I may still have a bit of fear in me! But Alice gave me—I suppose you call it a meditation session, which helped me to talk to my fear. Realise that it was there, and I could work with it. I know I have fears, but I am not going to let them stop me from moving forward. I just embrace my fears and move forward (take them with me on my journey), and not let them stop me going on my journey. I have put this into practice, and it helped me a great deal. Darren and I found it much easier for both of us to have sex.

Alice also told me that I can get valium from my doctor to relax the muscles. I think this helped me also, in that I knew there was another way to have sex, which took all this pressure off me and helped me a great deal. I am working with my fears.

Darren's Journal:

We had a very good week this week. Tina was very happy after your talk last Friday. She told me about the way she could go to the doctor for valium, if we were still having problems as time goes on. This reassurance helped, as on Sunday morning, after some nice foreplay, my penis entered with no problems, and I got to put it in further than before. I got to move around a good bit, and Tina also moved her hips to also participate. It felt very nice for me, and Tina did not have too much discomfort. A few more sessions of this, and I see no problem with me having an orgasm.

We both had a busy week this week with work and a relative to visit in the hospital. We did not get a chance to try again. I ended up having some time off today, and we were planning to try again. Tina's period started this morning, so we will wait a few days. Overall, we are both very happy and hopeful of a very good sexual relationship quite soon.

OUR MEETING TOGETHER:

I was pleasantly surprised and relieved that the couple had achieved full penetration of the vagina once this week. This was a major breakthrough. I could see from the journal entries that Tina had integrated the message about moving forward while feeling her fear. It was interesting that my suggestion about the possibility of using some valium had served to take pressure off her by making her feel as if there was a backup.

I coached the couple about maintaining this progress in the coming week and aiming to achieve ejaculation. I suggested to Darren that he stimulate himself to near the point of ejaculation before entering the vagina, in order to make it easier for Tina the first few times. I assured Tina that once the penis was deep in the vagina, it would be fun to move it around enough so that Darren could ejaculate. As they got used to having sex, they could then focus on increasing the enjoyment for both of them.

SESSION TWENTY THREE
OCTOBER 4TH

THE COUPLE WALKED IN, and, once they were seated, Darren announced that Tina had some good news to tell me. I turned to Tina who said with a beaming smile that this week the couple had had full sex with ejaculation! Tina was very tentative, as if she herself did not really believe it. I was delighted! I was also deeply grateful and relieved. Their achievement was also my achievement. We had all worked very hard together to reach this point. We spent time revelling in our success. Then I read the journals.

Tina's Journal:

Alice gave me another book to read called "Feel the Fear and Do it Anyway." It's a great read. I am enjoying it a great deal. It's all about fears. It tries to help you get over fear and says how to deal with your fear. These are some lines from the first two chapters I have read. "You can accept fear as simply a fact of life." Whatever happens to me, "I can handle it." "The only way to get rid of the fear of doing some-

thing is to go out and do it." Everybody feels fear when approaching something totally new in life. All of the above lines apply to me. And that's what I have been doing...facing my fears etc.

Things are going really well for Darren and me, and I am winning the battle against fear...the fear of sex! At last, I can say Darren and I are having sex---well, so Darren tells me, Ha! Ha!

I feel so happy, and so is Darren. I can't really believe it all. That it has happened at last. It was a long struggle to get to this place, but worth it all. And I deserve to be happy.

Darren's Journal:

This week was very good, as we had full sexual intercourse this morning. We both enjoyed it, and Tina did not find it too uncomfortable. I am very proud of Tina with all her progress and hard work. Our next step is to get used to sex and have lots of practice and for Tina to get more enjoyment from it. Also, with a bit of luck, we may get pregnant while we are practising.

OUR MEETING TOGETHER:

I congratulated the couple and said how pleased I was for them. I assured them that they would never go backwards now. The task ahead was simply for them to gradually get comfortable having sex and make it a regular part of their relationship. I suggested to Tina to begin taking supplements of Folic acid, just in case she became pregnant. She told me she was aware of protecting the unborn baby by taking folic acid, and she laughed as she told me she had been taking it for years! The couple were open to becoming pregnant right away, but I suggested to them that while we would work with whatever happened, it might be preferable to wait a few months until they had developed a comfortable sexual relationship. I jokingly suggested that I expected them to come in next March and tell me they were pregnant. I hoped that this gentle suggestion might convince their minds that they would get pregnant and would schedule it for March 2008---about five months away, giving the couple some time to enjoy their newfound sexuality.

SESSION TWENTY FOUR
11TH OCTOBER 2007

Tina's Journal:

Darren and I still find it hard to believe that the both of us are having a sexual relationship. Last week we spoke to Alice about the journey that we have come on! About the first night Alice met us and how fright-ened I was. I probably would have done anything not to enter "that room." That room for months af-terwards was my refuge. Days I hated entering into that room, but I always came out of that room a more contented person and a more hopeful person about my future.

I can't say it was an easy journey, but I got to deal with a lot more than my sexual problem. I dealt with my relationship with my father, how to change nega-tive into positive. Alice helped me to get over the loss of Paddy and the way he passed away. I read the sex books, also the book by Betty J. Eadie about her near-death experience. Now I am reading "Feel the Fear but Do it anyway." All these books have helped me to grow as a person. I have had an affirmation written for me, and also a relaxation tape made for me. It's like I am starting out life like a new person. How glad I am now that I entered "that room!" Thank you so much, Alice. We are both on top of that hill at last.

Darren's Journal:

We had sex twice this week, after a busy weekend. On Wednesday morning, we woke early, and it went very well. No problems entering or ejaculating. Tina and I both enjoyed it. Wednesday night, we also tried more sex. It went very well, no problem entering, although Tina was a bit nervous that it might be sore after doing it in the morning. I did not get to ejaculate this time, as I think I stayed in a bit long, and Tina started to feel uncomfortable. We would have tried again this morning, but Tina had to be in work early.

The weekend was a bit hectic as we had a family occasion on Saturday. Then we had booked to do a water sport together on Sunday. Monday evening, we both were very sick and vomiting. We both had to stay off work on Tuesday. We were weak and tired. In the circumstances, I think we did very well this week on the sex front. We are both still a bit under the weather.

OUR MEETING TOGETHER:

The couple shared their joys and challenges with me. They wanted to have lots of sex now as if to make up for lost time. Life was infringing on this desire, e.g. work and social commitments as well as being ill. I encouraged them to be gentle with themselves and pointed out that it was impossible to make up for the six years of marriage when they did not have sex. Instead, I encouraged them to be fully in the present and really enjoy their newfound sexuality. I also reassured them that couples get better at sex with practice and that for a while yet they would be still learning about themselves and one another.

Tina then talked about how the couple had taken a new water-sport training weekend. She had been very afraid, but she had used her new learning about the nature of fear to enable her to feel the fear and go forward in spite of it. Darren was very surprised at how well she had met the challenges, and she herself agreed that in the past, she probably would have given in more easily to the fear and avoided the activity. She was pleased that she could extend her learning from our sessions to other areas of her life.

As always, we concluded our session by bringing light into their bodies, minds, and emotions to continue to support them on their journey.

SESSION TWENTY FIVE
19TH OCTOBER 2007

Tina's Journal:

This week I think we got to come to terms with the fact that we are having a sexual relationship. It's the first week since we started that we can believe it is happening. And it is no longer a dream but a reality. It's a dream that has come true at last. We keep saying to ourselves "We are doing it!"

It makes us both feel so good about ourselves. I still find it hard to believe after all those years of worry and the feeling of failure that it is all over now. I have become such a positive person about everything in my life, thanks to Alice's great help and also the wonderful books she has given me. I've become a real "Pollyanna."

It is reported that over 90% of what we worry about never happens. That means that our negative worries have about a 10% chance of being correct.

These last seven months have changed me so much. Only now, I feel the greatness of it all. It's like getting a second chance in life. The start of a wonderful beginning as husband and wife. Thanks to my wonderful husband, Darren, I am able to start my life again. His support to me over the years, especially in the last seven months, I will never forget. Thank you, Darren, for staying by my side. I love you. XXX.

Darren's Journal:

We had a very good week this week. We had full sex three times this week. We are very proud and happy with ourselves. Saturday night was our first. It went very well; easy to get in and no problem ejaculating. Tina gets a little uptight while we are doing foreplay, but, once the penis goes in, she relaxes.

On Tuesday night, we did it again and had no problems. Tina was still a little nervous to start off. During sex, Tina is starting to relax more and moving her hips, which is very nice for me, as we are very much together.

Thursday night, we also did it, and Tina was even more relaxed. We seem to be enjoying it even more. It is nice to be practicing and learning all about sex together.

OUR MEETING TOGETHER:

As expressed in the journals, the couple were progressing really well at this point. They were still getting accustomed to having sex together, but they were communicating very openly with one another, and they had a lovely attitude of openness to experimenting and learning. It had indeed been like a whole new life for them. Tina shared how the couple regularly looked at one another during the week and jokingly said: "We are doing it!" It was as if the reality was still sinking in. They could scarcely believe that after all the years of pain, they now had so much joy.

Tina had been reading regularly since coming to counselling, and she expressed her joy in all that she is learning. Often at night now as they went home from our sessions, they stopped at a bookshop in Wexford and browsed and ordered a book. Just like the visits to the beach in the summer, this was adding a dimension of pleasure to the trips. Coming to their counselling had now become an enjoyable night out together.

As always, I finished this session by having the couple visualise light coming into their minds, emotions and physical bodies, especially their sexual and reproductive organs. I noticed that, as a result of having listened to her meditation tape for many months, Tina was very quickly able to reach a deep level of relaxation once she closed her eyes. This would be a great resource for her throughout her life, as all types of meditation have wonderful benefits for the body, mind,

and spirit, and, once learned, the ability to meditate is usually maintained. It was another example of how the therapy
had benefitted Tina way beyond her goal of being able to
allow penetration of her vagina. She had gained awareness
and developed aspects of her own personality, which would
enrich her life in countless ways.

SESSION TWENTY SIX
25TH OCTOBER 2007

Tina's Journal:

This week was a good week, taking all things that were happening into account. I think we did okay. A family member of mine who has been ill came home from hospital on Friday, which is great news. The patient is staying with us still, so we didn't have the house to ourselves, which can be hard at times because you become so used to your own space, etc.

But we managed to have sex Sunday morning, which was lovely. We also tried on Tuesday night, but it did not really work out. Also, Wednesday night, we got to have sex, but Darren did not get to ejaculate. I know he was a bit disappointed about that, but it was late, and we were both tired. We have been having people call to the house to see our patient. I got my period this morning, but I am looking forward to when it is over to start having sex again. We both are enjoying the sexual relationship we have now. It's all new to us and all a learning process, which will get better the more we learn etc.

Darren's Journal:

We had another good week this week. On Sunday morning we made love. It went very well, and we both enjoyed it. After the sex, I gave Tina an orgasm with my finger, so we were both very happy. Tina's relative who has been ill was still with us, and it did not affect us.

On Wednesday night, we tried again, and I put my finger in, but did not manage to put in my penis. Tina was worried about the patient who is with us. Thursday night, we tried again, even though Tina was still worried and not that interested in sex. I got to put in my finger and then the penis. I stayed in for about ten to fifteen minutes, but I did not manage to ejaculate. We stopped and decided it was better to wait for a better day or night. Tina's period is also near, and she feels a bit hormonal. We are both looking forward to more sex and practice after Tina's period.

OUR MEETING TOGETHER:

Even though the week had been challenging for the couple, with a family member staying in their home, they were both pleased that they had managed a reasonable level of sexual expression. I assured them that it is normal for stress in either partner to affect the sexual relationship. This is simply a fact of life that couples have to negotiate. I have constantly encouraged them to allow their experience to happen and to refrain from judging themselves or getting upset if sometimes the outcome was less than they would like. I was pleased that they seemed to be able to take this attitude of acceptance towards their sexual performance.

The couple had been having sex for four weeks now, and I discussed with them their feelings about lessening the frequency of our meetings to once a fortnight. Up to now, apart from holidays, they had been attending every week. I was conscious of the commitment to them every week of travelling a long journey and paying for the session. While I felt that they could still benefit from support from me, I also wanted to be as fair as possible to them. For me as a therapist, this is another judgement call, I regularly make. I try to ensure people get the support they need, but I discourage long-term dependence on me. Each client ultimately decides how long the therapeutic relationship should last, but often this decision is made in discussion with me.

The couple were pleased to reduce their contact to twice a month. They saw it as a compliment and as an acknowledgement of their progress that they had less need for me. I reassured them that within the fortnight if they ever had a crisis they were most welcome to phone me and bring forward their appointment. I also suggested that for a while longer they would continue to write a weekly journal to record their experiences and feelings.

SESSION TWENTY SEVEN
8TH NOVEMBER 2007

Tina's Journal 2nd November 2007:

Had my period over the weekend, so it was Monday morning before we had sex. It was the bank holiday, so we had plenty of time together before and after sex, which was lovely. We both enjoyed it a lot. Then it was Thursday morning when we had sex again. I was so pleased with myself. I am very happy in myself when we have sex. I am so proud of the progress we have both made. I am so delighted to be me, which is such a change!

When I think about my life this time last year, I think about how unhappy I was inside, keeping this problem to ourselves and not doing anything about it. It was eating away at both of us. It was so unhealthy for our marriage. We are both like two new people now. Getting a second chance in life! It's great, and I love it!

Tina's Journal 8th November:

This week we tried sex over the weekend on Sunday morning. But we just could not do it. It was just not working out for us. So we said we wouldn't get too worked up about it and enjoy our Sunday together. We had a lovely day. We went for a spin on our bikes etc. But I know the two of us were a bit disappointed about not having sex in the morning.

We were going to try Monday night, but the two of us were tired and fell asleep. Then Tuesday morning, we said we would try again, and we had sex. We were both so pleased with ourselves and so happy about it. We also had sex on Wednesday night. We had a nice night. It wasn't easy at first, but we did it. Both of us are happy that we had sex. It puts the two of us in great form. I am totally enjoying sex. I can't believe I said that!

Darren's Journal: 2nd November 2007.

We had another good week this week. On the bank holiday Monday morning, we made love. We enjoyed it, and had quite a bit of fun doing it.   I also got to give Tina an orgasm after the sex, and I had no problems ejaculating. Thursday morning, we also enjoyed more sex, and again no problems ejaculating.

Darren's Journal: 8th November 2007.

We had another very good week. Over the weekend, we planned on plenty of lovemaking. It did not go quite to plan, as Tina was very busy with both her parents ill. Her dad had to go to the doctor and hospital on Saturday, so Tina of course looked after him. He is okay, but he just does a bit of worrying about himself.

We tried sex on Sunday morning, but I found it too hard to get in, so we left it for another day. Tuesday morning, we managed to have sex again, and we both enjoyed it very much. On Wednesday night, we also had sex. It took a little while to get in, but then it went very well. We are back on track again.

OUR MEETING TOGETHER:

The couple had plenty of sexual contact in the two previous weeks and came into me in very good form. Sometimes their sex went really well and both achieved great enjoyment from it. Other times, it was a little more difficult, but the couple were able to discuss this with me and were taking it in their stride. I was noticing that Darren was occasionally having difficulty ejaculating, and I assured him that this happens to every man at times. I explored with him what might be contributing to this. Darren admitted that he was feeling under pressure to have sex in the days coming up to Tina's ovulation, because he would really like to have a baby. Tina said that at this point she was just so overjoyed to be having sex that she really was not concerned about getting pregnant yet. Certainly, she wanted a baby, but she was happy to enjoy the sexual contact in the meantime.

I spoke with the couple about pregnancy and assured them that research indicates that a high percentage of couples who have regular sex get pregnant within twelve months. I

encouraged Darren to relax and enjoy his time with Tina, as they will never get this time back, and once they have a baby, they will be sharing their lives with another human being. I stressed that, even though the couple were in their mid thirties, another few months would make little difference to Tina's prospects of having a healthy baby and normal delivery.

I suggested to the couple that, with their permission I would like to write to the referring G.P., to tell him they were now having full sexual relations. The couple said they would like to go and see the G.P. to thank him for his help. I thought this was a great idea. They said they would do this in the fortnight before I saw them again.

SESSION TWENTY EIGHT
23RD NOVEMBER 2007

Tina's Journal 15th November:

Last week, we talked about having a baby and how Darren is so excited and wants to have a baby straight away. Alice told Darren there was no rush and to just enjoy having sex for now. It's great that Darren is excited about having a baby. That has not hit me yet, not the way it has hit Darren. I am just so delighted with having sex. I can't believe it. I feel very fulfilled and closer to Darren.

I feel great after having sex—a happy and loved feeling, a feeling of warmth etc. It feels so right. I knew I was missing something in my life, and now I found it—sex! I feel like couples that have been trying hard to have children and get pregnant. That's the feeling I have with having sex. The feeling of wishing and longing for something that your heart desires! Then one day you get it.

We had sex this week on Saturday morning before work. Also Wednesday morning before work. We both enjoyed the two mornings. I made an appointment to see the doctor on Monday morning to thank him etc.

Tina's Journal 23rd November:

I went to see my doctor on Monday morning. I thanked him for all his help and told him we are hav-

ing sex. He wanted to know did I need anything and if I did just to call in. I also got to thank Sally the nurse for all her kindness etc. She was delighted to hear we were having sex. I found it hard to go back to the doctor's, but I was very glad I went back to thank them.

Darren and I had sex Friday morning. On Saturday morning, we tried twice, and again on Sunday night. We had sex each time, but Darren was not able to ejaculate. I know that he was a bit put out by this, but we looked on the positive side of it. We had sex, which is still a major achievement for the both of us. We tried again on Wednesday morning before work, and Darren was able to ejaculate. We were both so happy with ourselves. Lucky we did it, because I got my period on Wednesday.

Darren's Journal 16th November:

This week, we had full sex on Saturday and Wednesday mornings. It went very well, and we both enjoyed the two occasions. On Friday morning, we tried again, but, on this occasion, I was not able to ejaculate. We did not worry too much and decided to wait until over the weekend to try again.

Darren's Journal 23rd November:

The weekend did not go that well for me. We tried on Saturday morning. We made love, but I could not reach orgasm. I am not sure, but I may have been trying too hard or conscious that, on Friday morning, I did not manage it. We tried twice on Saturday morn-

ing. On Sunday night, we also tried again. No problems getting in or anything like that, but, again, I did not orgasm. On Wednesday morning, we managed to have full sex with orgasm. We had left it for a few days, and this may have helped. I had also relaxed more and just enjoyed the sex more, and everything was ok. It was a great relief that everything was ok. Tina's period came afterwards that morning, so we will try again over the weekend.

OUR MEETING TOGETHER:

The couple had full sex with ejaculation three times since our last session. On three other occasions, they had penetrative intercourse, but Darren did not ejaculate. I invited Darren to use this session to talk about how he was feeling. At this point in the therapy, it seemed that Darren was temporarily struggling, while Tina was enjoying the fruits of her efforts over the previous months. I was aware that while I always involved Darren in the couple sessions, the focus was usually more on Tina. In this session, I tried to meet Darren's needs and to understand what was now happening for him.

As Darren spoke about himself with Tina and myself, two main reasons for his anxiety became apparent. For years, Darren had been "minding" Tina and avoiding causing her any sexual discomfort. Even though Tina was progressing well at this point, Darren was still protecting her and was very conscious of not thrusting his penis too forcibly inside of her. It seemed that this focus on being gentle may have prevented him from letting go sufficiently to ejaculate. Keeping control generally inhibits sexual enjoyment! I spoke with Darren about this and encouraged him to relax and enjoy himself. Tina also assured him that she wanted him to relax and stop worrying about her.

It also seemed that now that Tina is functioning better and the couple are actually having sex, Darren is putting pressure on himself to have everything perfect. I assured him that perfection is an impossible goal in any human activity, and in relation to sexuality, very few couples have continuously great sex without the occasional moment of awkwardness or poor performance. I encouraged Darren

to allow himself to relax and "be average." Then I offered
to write an affirmation to help him with his current anxiety. He was enthusiastic in his response, and I wrote the
following for him: "I relax and enjoy all my sexual contact
with Tina. I let go of pressure and expectations and have
fun. All is well in my world." I suggested that he repeat the
affirmation morning and evening and several times during
the day and see how it felt to him. Then I finished with
our usual visualisation to bring light into every part of the
couple's being and relating.

Session Twenty Nine
7th December 2007

Tina's Journal 30th November:

We had a lovely week together. The last visit to Alice, Darren spoke about how feels when the two of us have sex, but Darren does not get to ejaculate. I was glad that Darren got to speak to Alice about this. Alice told him this was okay, and that it happens many couples and that it is all part of a sexual relationship. It was so good for Darren to hear all this from Alice. Because we are now having sex, I think Darren has put himself under a lot of pressure to have full sexual intercourse every time we have sex. Alice gave Darren an affirmation, which I think is helping him a lot. He says his affirmations a few times a day.

This week, we had sex on Sunday morning, but not full sex. We had full sex on Monday morning, which was lovely. Also, we had full sex on Wednesday morning. We had sex on Thursday morning, and Darren was a bit disappointed because he did not get to ejaculate. But we are going to try over the weekend again and, of course, all next week. Darren and I are going away to a leisure centre with friends for a one-night stay, and I am looking forward to that—our first time in a hotel as a loving sexual couple.

Tina's Journal 7th December:

We had a lovely weekend and week. We did very well, having full sex three times this week. We had sex on Sunday morning, Monday night, and also Thursday night. We are both so happy with this, especially Darren. I think the affirmation has really worked for Darren. The both of us are really enjoying having sex together. It has brought us even closer, which we didn't think was possible.

I get this great warm feeling between us when we have sex. It's a lovely feeling. It's like no matter what happens in my life and around me, sex—having sex— puts all these things away. And I am in this bubble of warmth and love, and I think of nothing else. I am in this safe place—a haven of love. My affirmation has come true! I am a beautiful sexual woman, and I enjoy a comfortable and loving regular sexual relationship with my husband.

Darren's Journal 7th December:

"I relax and enjoy every sexual contact with Tina. I let go of all pressure and expectations and have fun. All is well in my world!"

The two weeks went very well. We had a lot of sexual contact. At the beginning of the fortnight, we did not have full sex, but I did not think too much or get worried. As the week went on, we had full and enjoyable sex. This week, we also had full sex on three days, and we are enjoying it much more. Tina is also making a lot of effort, and it is going much better. We seem to be getting the hang of it all. We both look forward to sex, and we both initiate sex at different times. I have been busy at work, but we also find time to be intimate, which is great. Sunday night, we had a meal and overnight at a hotel and leisure centre. We both enjoyed it a lot. We had a great time in the pool and sauna.

My affirmation seems to have done the trick. I am still saying it twice a day. Life is good for me.

OUR MEETING TOGETHER:

The couple were both in good form this week. They had a lovely relaxing weekend away with friends. Reading Tina's second journal entry touched my heart and brought a tear to my eye. How much she had grown in just six months! I told her how much I enjoyed reading it. She said she was now listening to her relaxation tape just once a week, but she was saying her affirmation regularly. I asked her to say it out loud for me in the session three times. She said it with conviction and told me that she really believed it now. It had become a truth, and we all rejoiced in that.

Tina also shared how she had gone alone two weeks ago to visit the doctor and nurse, and she had felt very good about herself for doing that. She had been nervous going in there, as it was her first time back since her smear test, but she was glad she had returned to say thanks. I complimented her on having the courage to do this, and I regarded it as a real confirmation of her progress.

Darren shared that he was more relaxed in himself and had felt supported by the affirmation. We spoke about having realistic expectations about sex and I also stressed that it is okay to sometimes engage in mutual touching which does not necessarily end in full sexual intercourse. The couple discussed the image of sex portrayed in the media, where it seems as if everyone is able to hop into bed and have glorious sex as often as desired. This image can be a disservice to people by setting up unrealistic and perhaps unachievable expectations and putting pressure on people to meet these targets. Because it seems as if everyone is having great sex, it can be more difficult for people with sexual problems to come forward and look for help.

The couple stated that they were so pleased that they asked for help, because they knew now that they were never going to tackle their problem alone. Their only regret was that they waited for nearly six years. However, they now felt that all those years in their marriage were like a distant memory. The more they had sex, the more it seemed as if it had always been part of their marriage, and they were living in the joy of their present circumstances.

SESSION THIRTY
21ST DECEMBER 2007

Tina's Journal 14th December:

I think I'm starting to let having sex sink in! I'm soaking it all up and letting it absorb in at last. I smile to myself when I think about it—that it's really happening to us. I look at everything so differently it's hard to explain. I've got meaning in my life. It has changed everything in my life all for the better. It makes me so happy and complete.

This week we had sex Sunday morning, which was a lovely way to start our Sunday. We had sex Wednesday night and also Friday morning. We enjoyed all three times a great deal.

Tina's Journal 21st December:

This week was a funny week of mixed feelings! Last week, I had a bit of an upset stomach, which I normally don't suffer from. Because of this, I thought that maybe I was pregnant—Darren was of course counting the months down. I kept telling Darren that I wasn't pregnant, but that did not stop him from hoping. I too was really hoping that I was pregnant, but I did not say this to Darren, as if he had me agreeing with him, he would be cracking open the champagne! For the first time in my life, I got to feel and know what it could be like to be pregnant. It was a wonder-

ful feeling. I had this inner happiness. I was delighted with myself. But a part of me also told me not to be thinking this way as I would be disappointed when my period came! Of course, my period came on Tuesday, and I was very disappointed and sad. Darren was great as always, and we look forward to 2008 and what it has to bring us.

We had sex on Monday night, and we look forward to our first Christmas ever having sex. What more could one ask for from Santa!

Darren's Journal 14th and 21st December:

We had another good two weeks, having sex four times in the fortnight before Tina's period came on Tuesday of this week. We are enjoying the sex, and, touch wood, we are having no problems with full sex and orgasm from my point of view. The affirmation is working: "I relax and enjoy every sexual contact with Tina. I let go of all pressure and expectation and have fun. All is well in my world."

We are looking forward to a great Christmas break with plenty of sex and time together. We both got a bit excited last week as Tina had a stomach pain for a few days and we thought it might be morning sickness. It was a false alarm, but it was nice to give us a bit of excitement, and we are looking forward to the real thing. We both really appreciate how far we have come, and we are so lucky to be at this stage of our relationship.

OUR MEETING TOGETHER:

As has become usual in our sessions at this point, there was an air of celebration in our conversation this evening a few days before Christmas. The couple were delighted about the progress they have made in their sexual relationship in 2007. They said that all they needed now to complete their joy would be for Tina to become pregnant. As always, I counselled patience and reassured them that a high percentage of couples who have regular sex find themselves pregnant within a twelve month period. I suggested to Tina that she refrain from going to the toilet straight after intercourse and simply lie in bed with Darren for a while, in order to maximise the opportunity for the sperm to move up the vagina towards the cervix. I also stated that I felt these months were very important to allow them to get comfortable having a sexual relationship, and I encouraged them to have a lovely Christmas together.

Toward the end of the session, we spoke about the possibility of my writing an account of their therapy with me.

The couple were enthusiastic and excited about this idea, and I encouraged them to think and speak about it over the holidays. I explained that I would need their written permission to write and publish the account, and that they would read my writing and agree to it before anybody else saw it.

SESSION THIRTY ONE
4ᵀᴴ JANUARY 2008

Tina's Journal 4ᵗʰ January:

We both had a really fab Christmas. We spent lots of time together and also with family and friends. We also spent a lot of time being sexual: Sunday morning, Monday morning, Wednesday night, Thursday night, Friday night, Saturday night, Sunday night, Monday morning, Wednesday morning, and Thursday morning. Only Sunday night and Wednesday morning was not full sex.

Looking at this, I think that all your hard work with us has paid off, Alice. If you could have told us back in March that our Christmas would be filled with so much sex, we wouldn't have believed you. May 2008 bring as much sex also!

At the last session, Alice spoke about writing about our journey over the last 9 months. Darren and I are both in favour of this idea, as we both think if any good can come out of what the both of us have been through for the last six years and especially the last 9 months, we would be delighted. We would like to show people that there is help out there.

Darren's Journal:

Christmas and the New Year went very well for Tina and I. We both had plenty of time off work, and we made the most of it, both sexually and just time en-

joyed together and with both of our families. Our target was to enjoy sex between Christmas and New Year, as this was the time for Tina to ovulate. We had full sex eight times and sex without ejaculation another two times. There is no need to say anymore, only we enjoyed our first Christmas having sex!

OUR MEETING TOGETHER:

The journals spoke for themselves! The couple had very frequent and enjoyable sex over the two-week Christmas break. They were very pleased with themselves. As always, I affirmed them and congratulated them on having dealt with their problems in 2007. I stated that the sexual problem is now a thing of the past and will never present itself in any other year.

As we began a new year working together, we marked the occasion by reviewing their progress. The couple spoke about their memories of our first session together, just over nine months ago. Darren said that when he made the appointment with me he had no idea how much effort the couple themselves would have to put in throughout the counselling.

I reassured him that this was a very common occurrence in that many clients have the notion that the therapist will solve the problem for them.

Tina then talked about the first appointment by sharing background information, which I had not heard before. She told me that when Darren had made their first appointment with me, she had then booked a dental appointment for earlier on the same day, in the hope that the dental appointment would take her mind off the deeper issue. She was therefore able to postpone thinking about our appointment until after seeing the dentist. Nevertheless, she was very afraid as Darren drove them to Curracloe. They had been early and stopped in a local pub for a cup of coffee. It was Friday evening, and Tina described how people were there having a drink after work, laughing and relaxing. She felt that she looked as if she was "going to a funeral," as she sat there long-faced and afraid. She was particularly fearful of what I would think of a woman of her age married for six years who had never had sex with her husband. She scarcely believed that there could be help for someone like her. She had always felt so alone with her problem which she had never shared with anyone, and now she was about to tell a stranger.

Tina continued describing their arrival at the first session, and said she did not want to go in and had no memory of walking up to the door. She told me that when I introduced myself to them, she felt trapped and cornered and wanted to leave. She began to cry and told Darren "I can't do this." She said she still does not know how I convinced her to stay for that first hour. She perceived herself as being in such a mess, crying and shaking etc, that she worried I might say she should "be signed into a centre." At the end of the session, she felt so much relief that she had finally told someone about her problem and that her dark secret had been brought into the light. Now nine months later, she was so delighted that with Darren's support she had been able to address her problems and move to such a new way of being in the world.

Session Thirty Two
18TH January 2008

Tina's Journal 12th January 2008:

This week went very well for us. We had sex Sunday night, Tuesday morning, Wednesday night, and Friday morning. Tuesday morning was the only time we did not have full sex. I got my period on Friday and Saturday. It was a few days early this month. Maybe that's a good thing, because if it was a few days late, we would be thinking maybe I was pregnant, which was what we were both hoping maybe this time. I know we are only having sex a few months, yet it doesn't stop us both from wishing we were pregnant. I do get a bit sad and low when my period starts. And I know that Darren gets a bit disappointed also. I know we just have to wait and see what happens. Darren is so wonderful and supportive during it all. We have both wanted children for so long! Now that we are having sex, it has opened up a whole new world for us, the chance to have a child. We count down the months, and we get excited about the possibility of having a child. I know it is a journey that the both of us will have to travel. We have come such a long journey, another few miles won't kill us!

Tina's Journal 18th January:

We had sex on Wednesday morning and this morning. We both enjoyed each time. I even missed sex, while I had my period over the weekend. Our Sunday was not the same. Ha Ha! Darren was very pleased to hear me say that I missed sex. It's starting to become part of our lives, which is great. I am back on track again after my period, looking forward and hoping that this might be the time we get pregnant. We are both enjoying every moment we spend together and apart, and we both love these feelings we are having for one another.

Darren's Journal 18ᵗʰ January:

We had another good fortnight. The first week we had sex three times, and the middle time I did not have an orgasm, but we did not worry about that. The last time we had sex, Tina's period started. It was a little early. We were a bit disappointed, as we were hoping that we might be pregnant, after all the sex at Christmas. This week we had sex on Wednesday morning and this morning. All went very well, and we both enjoyed it very much.

OUR MEETING TOGETHER:

At this stage in our therapy, the couple were progressing very well and were having a very regular sexual relationship. In their journals, when they have said they did not have "full" sex, what they meant in fact is that they had sexual intercourse, but Darren did not ejaculate. While I noticed this, I chose not to focus too much on this in our meetings, as I was hoping that more sexual experience and a growing knowledge of one another's bodies would lessen its occurrence.

Since we had addressed the couple's main issues and to a large extent Tina and Darren had now met their goals for the therapy, my role had become one of offering support and encouragement. The sessions were easier and less intense. The hour together provided the couple with an opportunity to reflect on and share their progress. They could also talk about any other issues that were arising in their lives, and in every session, their desire to get pregnant was high on the agenda. It seemed that being able to talk with me about getting pregnant was important to them. I provided a balanced and reassuring viewpoint, and I hope that this served to lessen their anxiety. I had seen in my work with other couples over the years that a strong desire and anxious efforts to get pregnant are unhelpful in actually achieving that goal. When couples relax and trust in the universe, they more easily become pregnant.

I continuously encouraged Darren and Tina to enjoy their precious time together, and they seemed to be doing that. They regularly expressed to me how their sexual relationship had brought a new level of joy and love into their marriage. They were having more fun together inside and outside the bedroom. A very good marriage had become even better.

SESSION THIRTY THREE
1ST FEBRUARY 2008

Tina's Journal 1st February:

Darren and I had a nice two weeks. We had sex five times, and only once it wasn't full sex. Sex has really become part of our lives. It's hard to believe how it is becoming so natural to us both. It is as if we were doing it all our lives. I even find it hard to remember what life was like before we started having sex. It is as if the memory has vanished, which is a good feeling as we want to keep moving forward and forget about all the past. The future is all I care about now. The past I can't change, but the future I can look forward to. And be positive and strong to deal with what lies ahead. With Darren by my side, I can deal with anything that may lie ahead. This has made us both so much stronger as people, and our relationship has also been strengthened.

Darren's Journal 1st February:

We had another good fortnight. The first week I was very busy in work, and also I had to work a few evenings. We had sex five times, but one of the times I did not have an orgasm. It was one morning last week, and I was very tired and also in a hurry to work. We did not try for long, as we knew things were not working out that morning. Once I got back to myself, we had no problems. The other four times went very well, and we enjoyed them.

167

Our Meeting Together:

It was St. Brigid's Day, and Tina brought me a lovely St. Brigid's Cross, which she had bought from a friend in support of a local charity. I was delighted to have it, and I appreciated her thoughtfulness."

For the first time in a while, I asked the couple to describe the exact details of their foreplay and lovemaking as it was at this point. Though Tina was more relaxed and engaged during the sexual intercourse and Darren was pleased that she now moved her hips in a natural and spontaneous way, Darren still seemed to be taking most of the responsibility for getting Tina ready for intercourse. First the couple kissed and hugged and touched one another. Then Darren masturbated himself, then put his finger with the KY Jelly into Tina's vagina, and then inserted his penis.

I encouraged Tina to participate more, and suggested that they now engage in more mutual foreplay, in which she will stimulate Darren as he is using his hand on her vagina. I also suggested that as a homework assignment Tina would just one time stimulate Darren to the point of orgasm. Darren said that he would like this. Tina said that she had no hesitation in doing it as she saw that Darren was still taking a lot of responsibility. I said I felt this would also make it easier for Darren to orgasm, as the lovemaking would be more shared. I explained that Darren had been taking care of Tina for a long time, and now he could let go of this role and allow Tina to also take care of him.

I was due to go away on holidays, so it would be three weeks before the couple saw me again. I requested that they would see how this interval felt to them, and if they were comfortable, we could then move to a three week space between all the sessions. Obviously, if any problem arose during the three weeks, they could simply phone me and arrange to come sooner. They both seemed happy with this agreement.

SESSION THIRTY FOUR
22ND FEBRUARY 2008

Tina's Journal 18th February 2008:

I am not getting upset this time about having my periods, because life is too short to be feeling sad. I know it's an important thing for us, but it won't make us feel any better being sad. It just won't help us get pregnant. I just want to feel positive about the next time, and I will work hard to achieve our goal. We can only do so much, and the rest is in God's hands.

Darren and I have had a good two weeks of sex after my periods. We had sex eight times. We are both really enjoying sex and being close to one another. I still find it hard to remember what our life was like before we had sex. It is as if we have been having sex for years, and it gets better each time we have sex. I find great comfort, warmth, and love every time we have sex. I feel very safe. It feels as if nothing else matters. Everything is put aside. I have no worries or fears while we are having sex, etc. It has become a very special act for me, and I am loving every minute of it. "All is well in my world."

Darren's Journal 22nd February:

We had three very good weeks. The first week was Tina's period. We had full sex with orgasm on the Sunday morning, Monday night, Wednesday night, Friday morning, Sunday morning, Monday morning, Wednesday morning, and Thursday night. I am very

*pleased as I seem to be having no problem reaching
orgasm now. Tina is also doing the foreplay on me,
which is a lot more intimate and fun. We are enjoying
regular sex and not getting too excited about getting
pregnant. We are letting nature take its course.*

OUR MEETING TOGETHER:

As agreed at our previous session, Tina had participated
more in the couple's foreplay, and on the eight occasions they
had sex, Darren had reached orgasm without any difficulty.
Tina was really enjoying their sexual intercourse. She did
not have an orgasm during sex, and she preferred Darren to
manually stimulate her to orgasm after intercourse. They
were doing this whenever Tina desired it. Tina regularly
initiated sex now, which was very pleasing to Darren. All
in all, their sexual relationship seemed to be developing
beautifully.

Tina shared her joy in her current sexual relationship with
Darren. She said that having sex has made everything in her
world seem good. She expressed her appreciation at being
able to speak openly with myself and Darren about her de-

veloping sexuality and also spoke of her regret about all her years of silence and isolation, in which she thought she was the only person in the world with sexual difficulties. I assured her that she was not alone, and that, in my own experience very few people actually speak with anyone about their sexuality. Even women who have close friendships with one another often speak about everything except their sexual experiences and relationships. This lack of appropriate openness about sexuality leads to a feeling of isolation, in which people think: "I am unusual."

I explained to the couple that the times in my own life when I have shared openly with other people about my sexual history, feelings and experiences have been in training groups with other psychotherapists. To begin with, people are always shy and fearful about the topic. As some people have the courage to open up, others join in, and the discussion tends to deepen and lead to great a great sense of relief and support for one another. The single most important thing I have learned from such groups is that we all need to accept our humanity and our imperfection in relation to sex. Very few people have "perfect" sexual histories or "perfect" sexual experiences. Most people carry some sexual hurts. Those who are "whole" sexually are the unusual ones. The rest of us journey toward wholeness. So we need to love ourselves and not take it all too seriously. We need to just do our best in whatever relationship we choose to be in.

Session Thirty Five
13th March 2008

Tina's Journal:

We had sex six times the past three weeks, which was lovely each time. We are getting better at it, and also loving it more and more. My period came two days late this time. Since it has been coming early in recent months, I hoped that this time I might be pregnant. But this did not happen. Yet I know I will be writing in this book someday soon: "I am pregnant." I am really looking forward to this happy day.

I didn't tell Darren that I was two days late, as I know he would be so excited. Darren would make a fab father, so kind and full of love. Sometimes I feel like we are in limbo waiting for this wonderful thing to happen to us, knowing that this baby would change our world and complete our lives. It would give meaning to our lives. The unknown of whether we can or can't have a child is sometimes hard. I know it can't happen overnight. It will take time. I know I should be so grateful for how far we have come on this journey. And I am so grateful, but I can't help wanting more. Wanting a little baby Darren, ha, ha!

Darren's Journal 13th March:

I read in a book about Reiki healing by Kathleen Milner the following statement, which I like: "I am at peace with myself and the world. Problems and challenges facing me are no longer disturbing, because I

*have made contact with my true source of intelligence
and power. I am guided to do the right thing at the
right time."*

*The last three weeks were good for Tina and me. We
had plenty of sex and no problems. Tina's period
came last week. On Monday I had a small operation,
and everything is fine except for a small inflammation
of the bladder. I recovered well and we tried sex on
Wednesday night. No orgasm for me, but it was a bit
early after the operation, and I still had some soreness
when going to the toilet. This morning, we had full
sex with orgasm. We were very happy as Friday is
day ten of Tina's cycle, so we want to keep trying for
a baby.*

OUR MEETING TOGETHER:

As the couple had developed and gradually improved their

sexual relationship, Tina had become a much more positive

person. I was delighted to read in her journal her belief that

she would soon write "I am pregnant." I encouraged her to

hold this vision and trust that it would happen when the time

was right. I also said that I thought the little baby who had

Tina and Darren as parents would be very fortunate indeed!

The couple said they would love to have an affirmation to

help them to be positive about getting pregnant. After some

consideration, I decided it was best to write two individual affirmations to suit their individual needs. They were both wholehearted in their acceptance of the statements, which they transcribed into their journals.

Having had a medical investigation during the week, Darren took part of the session to speak about a few minor health concerns. He had always been very health-conscious and goes for regular check-ups as there was some history of illness in his family. He was on no medication, but looked after himself by eating well. He had always encouraged Tina to look after her health also.

My writing of this book was part of the therapy now, and the couple regularly asked me how the writing was progressing. At the end of this session, I gave the couple a copy of my account of their therapy to read and correct and discuss with me at our next meeting. As always, they were enthusiastic about the book and pleased to see and hold the pile of printed pages.

Session Thirty Six
4ᵀᴴ April 2008

Tina's Journal 4ᵗʰ April:

*Darren and I had a nice three weeks. We both en-
joyed lots of sex. We had sex eight times over the
last three weeks. Also I got my period during the last
week. It came three days early this time. Of course, I
had the usual feelings of disappointment and sadness,
but I don't stay that way for long. I always believe
there is a reason for everything, and maybe someday
it will all make sense to me!*

*I found the affirmation that Alice wrote me in the
last visit great. It gave me hope to believe that it can
be possible for me to have a baby. It's very positive
and powerful, and I enjoy saying it over and over. It
goes as follows: "In the near future when the time is
right, I find myself pregnant. The baby grows at a
perfect rate, and I fell so healthy and happy, and in
nine months I give birth to a perfect baby. All is well
in my world."*

*I find now that Darren is more attentive and helpful
around the house etc. It has changed him so much.
He is much more happy and content with himself and
also with me. And I myself feel more content and
happy in myself.*

Darren's Journal:

> *I love my affirmation from the last session: "In the near future, I father a wonderful healthy baby. I am so proud of myself, and I love being a daddy."*
>
> *I really enjoyed Alice's book on our story. I am very proud of Tina and all she went through over the last year. As I write this, it is a year since we started to visit Alice. The counselling has really helped, and we both now know we were never going to overcome our sexual problem without the help of a counsellor. We were lucky to be sent to Alice, as we got on very well with her, and she had a lot of experience in different areas which helped, as Tina had a few different barriers to overcome.*
>
> *We are both very positive about getting pregnant, and we are saying our new affirmations. Tina's period came on Saturday, but we did not let it bother us, although as always we were hopeful that this could be the month. We are not being selfish by wanting more. We are really enjoying the sex regularly and would like if we could be blessed with a child, if it is meant to be! We know we just have to be patient and keep trying and praying.*

OUR MEETING TOGETHER:

Most of this session was spent in conversation about the couple's desire to get pregnant. Darren had some questions for me about the different stages of pregnancy and how best to support Tina. The couple knew some people who had experienced the grief of miscarriage and spoke about their fears about this. I explained that a high percentage of first time pregnancies end in miscarriage, and while it is good to know the facts, it is important to stay positive and hopeful in their outlook about getting pregnant and having a full-term baby. I also stressed that most couples who experience miscarriage go on to have healthy babies.

I had cut an article out of a magazine about what foods to eat and not to eat during pregnancy, and I gave this to Tina. She was very interested in it and pleased to have it. I also lent the couple a video about the development of a baby, including the nervous system. They were grateful for this, as neither had a background knowledge of biology.

It was a year now since I first met Darren and Tina, and what a journey we had had together! I shared with them what an honour it had been for me to work with them and my joy in their growth both as individuals and as a couple. They expressed their gratitude for my help and for the amazing learning they have achieved. They spoke about the growth of love in their relationship and a newfound unity and contentment. They expressed their excitement about the book and their hope that it would reach out the hand of encouragement to others to seek help. They were now two different people than those I first met a year ago, and I too had grown.

FINAL SESSION
11TH JULY 2008

Tina's Journal 11th July:

Things are going well for Darren and I at the moment. We are enjoying a regular sexual relationship with one another. It has become such a part of our lives. It is like another food for our body. We need sex to live a healthy and happy life. And I feel so healthy and happy. The sex gets better the longer we are having it. It is like a good wine that improves with time. And it is gradually changing my life for the better. I have come a long way since last year, and "all is well in my world."

Darren and I have been enjoying every minute together. It has been the best summer we could ask for. We are both so much happier in ourselves and with one another. What more could anyone ask for—well maybe a little baby! We are so happy with all we have done and are doing to have a baby, and we are hopeful that we will have a baby soon. We don't take anything for granted, and we live every day to the full. This is "the way life is meant to be."

Darren's Journal:

Tina and I are both doing well, and we had very regular and enjoyable sex over the summer months. The more we do it, the more comfortable and enjoyable it is for us. I had a sperm test, just to reassure myself that all is well, and the results showed plenty of good quality sperm. Tina is now doing some complimentary therapies to help her get pregnant. We are both thinking positively about pregnancy and also praying, and hopefully in the near future we will get a surprise.

OUR MEETING TOGETHER:

The couple and I had agreed to have one final check-in session in the middle of the summer. This would mark the termination of our work together and give us a chance to say goodbye. I was once again struck by how beautiful Tina looked—so full of joy and vitality. Their sexual relationship was now very comfortable, spontaneous, and regular. They both spoke about their desire to be pregnant, and I shared my progress on publishing the book. Their waiting to get pregnant and my waiting to publish the book seemed to be kind of a parallel process, and we were all very supportive of one another. Since we live quite far apart and would be unlikely to ever meet, we agreed that the couple would inform me when they got pregnant, and, of course, I assured them that they would be the first to receive a signed copy of COMPLETE UNION.

AFTERWORD

JUST A COUPLE OF WEEKS AFTER OUR FINAL MEETING, the couple phoned me to say that they were expecting a baby. We had a joyful telephone conversation and shared our delight. This was the perfect ending to our story for which we had all hoped. It has been an honour to work with this couple, and I am deeply grateful for their generosity in allowing me to write the book and include their personal journals. I sincerely hope that the writing will be of help to many other people. My most pressing message to my readers is to always seek help for personal difficulties, no matter what their nature. There are a wide variety of therapies available nowadays, and it is well worth the effort to seek out and find the therapy most suitable for you. No matter what your problems, there are others who share them, and there is no need to suffer in isolation and silence. The first step takes the most courage, but the rewards are so abundant.

Appendix I

Complete transcript of the tape made for Tina.

"Now, Tina, this is a tape to help you to relax and to relax very very deeply. And each time you listen to this tape now, it is going to help you to open your mind to have a very positive attitude about your own body and about your sexuality and particularly about your sexual relationship with Darren. And this tape will play an important part now in helping your mind to know that you can have a very successful sexual relationship with your husband and that in time you can grow to enjoy that relationship and have children and whatever else you want from the relationship. So now we begin with the relaxation and you can keep your eyes open for a moment now and look up at a spot on the ceiling. I am going to count from ten to one, and, with every descending number, I'd like you to slowly blink your eyes. Slowly close and then open your eyes as in slow motion with every number. Ten...nine...eight...seven...six...five...four...three... two...one... Very good, Tina. Now you can close your eyes, and you can keep them closed all the while I'm talking to you.

That little exercise was just to relax your eyelids, and right now in your eyelids, there is probably a feeling of relaxation, perhaps a comfortable, tired feeling, or a pleasant, heavy sensation. And whatever the feeling is right now in your eyelids, just allow that feeling to multiply, to magnify, and to become greater. Allow your eyelids to become totally and pleasantly relaxed. This is something you can do now, Tina. Nobody else can do this for you. You are the one who does it. Just take your time now and completely and pleasantly relax your eyelids. And as you relax your eyelids, you can allow that feeling of relaxation that is now in your eyelids to flow outwards in imaginary waves or ripples. Allow a feeling of relaxation to go outward to your entire facial area. Just think about relaxing your face now Tina. Then, allow a feeling of relaxation to go outward to your entire head area. Just think about relaxing your head. Enjoy the relaxation going to your neck and shoulders, down the arms, and into your hands. Welcome a wonderful feeling of relaxation going down your entire body, to your legs and your feet, all the way down to your toes, completely and pleasantly relaxing your entire body. And you slow down a little bit. Allow yourself to slow down just a little bit. Then, as we go along you can slow down a little bit more.

In a moment now, I'm going to count downward once again from ten to one, and, this time, as you hear every descending number, just feel yourself slow down a little bit more with every number, and then, at the number one, you can enter your own natural level of relaxation. I will count rapidly now: ten, nine, eight, going deeper into relaxation now, seven, six, five, much much deeper, four, three, two, and one. You are now at your own natural level of relaxation. You are completely aware at every level of your mind, even though your body feels so relaxed. You are in complete control. At this level of relaxation or at any other level, you can give yourself positive mental suggestions, suggestions that your inner mind can accept and act upon in a positive manner, suggestions that are designed for your success, to achieve your goal and ideal of having a pleasing sexual relationship with your husband. See yourself now relaxed in mind

*and in body. This is something that you want. It is
here and it is now. Every breath that you take now,
every beat of your heart, every blink of your eyes,
and every sound outside and inside this room, including the sound of my voice, can all continue to take
you deeper into that pleasant and comfortable state
of relaxation.*

*In this special relaxation now, your deeper mind,
for your protection, takes note of what is happening
around you. So my suggestions, which are all for your
benefit, go directly to your subconscious mind. There
they are accepted, because these ideas are for your
benefit. These thoughts become firmly fixed, deep
in your inner mind, embedded so they remain with
you, helping you to begin to change those things you
want to change for your own sake. As you relax more
and more deeply now, your own self-healing forces
are switched on. Muscles, nerves, the very fibres of
your being rest and relax. Every system slows down,
breathing becomes more regular, heart beats more
smoothly, and digestion eases down. So your whole
being rests now. Healing forces, through your nervous
system, check every part of you, repairing, replacing,
and reenergising, soothing your mind and nerves. So
this relaxation enables you to feel fitter and stronger
in every way, your nerves stronger and steadier, your
mind serene and tranquil. Peace of mind and a deep
sense of well-being are experienced as you drift deeper
and deeper. These feelings stay with you. This new
found inner strength enables you to concentrate your
mind more keenly. Your memory improves, and you
feel more self assured, whatever you are doing. You
become so engrossed in what you are doing, what is
going on around you, that you have no need to think
of yourself. Your thoughts are directed outwards from
yourself to what you sense around you. Every day you*

become more relaxed, steadier, more settled mentally and physically. Your talents, abilities, all your special qualities begin to grow stronger and more rewarding. You recognise your own worth and become more aware of your own potential. You become more comfortable with your own physical body. You love that physical body, and you enjoy exploring it and sharing it with your husband. Your own natural warmth begins to show through. Therefore friends and acquaintances warm to you too. So your relationships get closer and more rewarding. As you become more comfortable with yourself and your body, you feel overall more self-confident. Your will-power, determination, and self-assurance grow and develop. You become more comfortable within yourself and within your surroundings. Day by day, life becomes more enjoyable and more fulfilling. You feel so much better within yourself and about yourself in every way.

And now, you know that you are a healthy active being, and therefore, as a healthy young woman, it is possible for you to discover your total sexual ability. With new understanding, you can develop a positive mental attitude toward all aspects of an exciting sexual life and a harmonious relationship with your husband by really understanding and being comfortable with yourself. You do not have to try to fit yourself into somebody else's mode. You can be happy knowing that you are you and that you are at ease and confident in your own body. You can trust your feelings and inner judgement, as you discover and perfect your approach and style to sexual expression. Sexual growth is a learning and sharing experience, and, like love, it grows and develops over time. It becomes more beautiful and more fulfilling, as the weeks and months and years go by. You can calmly enjoy and appreciate each physical experience as an experience, without trying to analyse or compare, doubt or brag, beg or promise. All you really need to do is slow down and enjoy each experience, each part of the touching as a normal and enjoyable sensation.

Instinctively, your own body knows its own needs and in due time your body will fulfil them. By using pleasure as your guide, you discover and enjoy the desires and abilities that have been hidden in you up to now. You gain confidence and fulfilment by being creative in your passion. You gain new insight through observation and learning about yourself and your partner. You can ask yourself questions: "When is passion most enjoyable—day or night?" "Do I prefer dim lights or scented candles, music or silence?" "What is my body saying to me?" "How can I be more understanding of myself and of my partner?"

People in sexual relationships guide each other by learning to grow together. There are no rules to regulate what they choose to share. Lasting satisfaction is not a race to be won or a competition to see who finishes first. It is simply sharing your body in a pleasurable way with another person. For some, the goal is not necessarily orgasm; the real goal is in tender touching, gentle words, and intimate embrace, for fulfilment sexually comes also from the heart. Often the greatest joy is not just in the doing, but by being playful together and truly enjoying each other and giving each other time in an intimate manner. The mutual giving and taking of affection is the secret of sexual harmony. Because there are no time limits, you can take hours for your light-hearted and your serious loving. Be at ease with yourself and with each other. Discuss your needs and wants and, just as important, what you enjoy giving and doing to the other person. Talk together freely about what you like and what you don't like. Touch lightly sometimes and touch deeply other times.

In your creative imagination, envision the kind of relationship that you want. See yourself balanced with equal amounts of give and take, doing and accepting, speaking and listening. Joy and happiness become the symbol and the rhythm of your life. Clearly visualise you and your partner sharing love and making love. Imagine yourself now with Darren, both of you naked in your bodies, having plenty of time and being relaxed together. Visualise yourself kissing, hugging, and gently touching one another in your private parts. Allow yourself to gently and gradually enjoy the experience of becoming more intimate together. See yourself now allowing yourself to orgasm by Darren touching you with his hands and then visualise yourself touching Darren so that he is also very turned on though not quite ready to orgasm. And then when you are ready, imaging yourself lying on your back with your head on the pillow with your legs and knees raised and holding your knees up so that you open up the private parts of your body. And then you gently put plenty KY jelly on to Darren and plenty KY Jelly into your own vagina. Put your finger in and rub in the KY Jelly. Then you visualise Darren lying on top of you, helping himself to stay up with his arms, so that he is not leaning heavily on you. Then gently allow him to push his penis in, gently in step by step a little bit at a time. Breathing deeply, allowing yourself to relax. Holding your pelvis back, tilting the pelvis back so the penis can go in the way which is easiest for it, tilting back towards the lower back. Visualise yourself feeling that, allowing that to happen, knowing that this is something you gradually get used to and gradually get to like. And then visualise Darren the first couple of times just putting his penis in perhaps half way but then gradually being able to put it in further, being able to move the penis back and forth inside of you, so that he gradually comes to the point where he orgasms inside of you. Just imagine now that lovely feeling of all that fluid inside of you, filling up your whole vagina, knowing that, in time, this experience can allow you to have a baby. And then imagine Darren moving out of you, and you both lie there and relax, feeling so good about yourself and so good about your own body, knowing that this is a normal experience for a woman to allow the man she loves to put his penis into her to fill her vagina with fluid. Feel the waves of pleasure in yourself, just knowing you have been able to do this. See yourself and Darren after lovemaking, lying on your bed nice and relaxed and so pleased with one another, and feeling very close to one another. Picture this afterglow now as the most pleasant part of all, an emblem of togetherness and peace. Feel yourself hum with satisfaction and fulfilment and a real sense of joy and pleasure in yourself. You are pleased that you both enjoyed one another. In your mind, you hear yourself or your partner saying, "Wow, that was wonderful." And it was. Feel this now as already accomplished, and be thankful for the sheer joy of being alive and together. And then visualise yourself so pleased as you go about your daily business that this part of your life is now working well. You feel healed and whole, like a woman who is healthy. You feel like a good wife, and you know that in time you can also be a good mother. You feel so pleased with yourself and so proud of the effort you have made to get to this point in your life.

In a moment now, I am going to count from one to five, and, at the count of five, you can open your eyes and return to full awareness, feeling so good and so positive about yourself, knowing that each time you listen to this tape, it will take you one step further toward the fulfilling, pleasurable, sexual relationship that you want to have with your husband. One... slowly, calmly, easily, returning to your full awareness once again. Two...every muscle and nerve in your body is feeling wonderfully good and relaxed. Three...from head to toe, you are feeling perfect in every way. Four...your eyes are beginning to feel sparkling clear, as if bathed in cool spring water. Five... you can open your eyes now, take a deep breath. Well done!"

BIBLIOGRAPHY

Bolduc, Henry Leo. *Self-Hypnosis: Creating Your Own Destiny*. Virginia, U.S.A.: Adventures into Time, 1992.

Chaplin, J.P. *Dictionary of Psychology*. New York: Dell Publishing Co., Inc., 1968.

Chopra, Deepak. *Creating Health: Beyond Prevention toward Perfection*. London: Grafton Books, 1987.

Covington, Stephanie S. *Awakening Your Sexuality*. Minnesota: Hazelden, 1991.

Eadie, Betty J. *Embraced by the Light*. New York: Bantam Books, 1992.

Jeffers, Susan. *Feel the Fear and Do it Anyway*. London: Random House, 1991.

Keaney, Joseph E. *Course Material of the Institute of Clinical Hypnotherapy and Psychotherapy*. Cork, Ireland: Undated.

Mace, David. *Sexual Difficulties in Marriage*. Rugby,
England: The National Marriage Guidance Council,
1972.

McCall, Davina, and Naik, Anita. *Let's Talk Sex*.
London: Channel 4 Books, 2007.
Used with permission of the Random House Group Ltd

Milner, Kathleen Ann. *Reiki and Other Rays of Touch
Healing*. U.S.A.: Healing Arts Series, 1993.

Weiss, Brian. *Only Love is Real*. London: Piatkus, 1996.

Winston, Professor Robert. *Getting Pregnant: The
Complete Guide to Fertility & Infertility*. London: Pan
Books Limited, 1993.

About the Author

Alice McLoughlin was born in South Kilkenny in 1960. After her Leaving Certificate, she obtained a scholarship to the U.S.A., where she studied for six years and graduated with a B.A. Degree in Psychology and English in 1982 from Immaculata University, and a Master of Science Degree in Counselling and Human Relations in 1985 from Villanova University. Never aspiring to be an emigrant abroad, Alice returned to Ireland and worked full time in the field of addiction treatment for eleven years. Then, in 1996, she set up her own private counselling practice and continues to work with a wide range of clients.

Over the years, Alice has added various training courses to her repertoire of skills, including a Diploma in Advanced Hypnotherapy from the Institute of Clinical Hypnotherapy and Psychotherapy in 1997 and a Post-Graduate Certificate in Counselling Supervision from Trinity College Psychology

Department in 2004. She is an accredited member and supervisor with The Irish Association for Counselling and Psychotherapy and The Irish Association of Alcohol and Addiction Counsellors.

Alice is married to Patrick and lives and works in the seaside village of Curracloe, County Wexford, Ireland.